Sara J. Ahmed

Evaluating the Framing of Islam and Muslims Pre- and Post-9/11

Sara J. Ahmed

Evaluating the Framing of Islam and Muslims Pre- and Post-9/11

A Contextual Analysis of Articles Published by the New York Times

VDM Verlag Dr. Müller

Imprint

Bibliographic information by the German National Library: The German National Library lists this publication at the German National Bibliography; detailed bibliographic information is available on the Internet at http://dnb.d-nb.de.

Cover image: www.purestockx.com

Publisher:
VDM Verlag Dr. Müller Aktiengesellschaft & Co. KG, Dudweiler Landstr. 125 a, 66123 Saarbrücken, Germany,
Phone +49 681 9100-698, Fax +49 681 9100-988,
Email: info@vdm-verlag.de

Produced in USA and UK by:
Lightning Source Inc., La Vergne, Tennessee, USA
Lightning Source UK Ltd., Milton Keynes, UK
BookSurge LLC, 5341 Dorchester Road, Suite 16, North Charleston, SC 29418, USA

ISBN: 978-3-639-00332-1

Table of Contents

List of Tables

For Adil
For supplying me with infinite amounts of
Support and Love during the research and writing of this study,

For my parents, Syed Jawaid & Shahida Ahmad
For instilling in me the desire to learn and
Always encouraging my free-spirited endeavors.

Chapter 1 – Introduction

The importance of media as a vehicle for communicating information is blatantly evident when placed in the context of a post-9/11 world. On 9/11/2001, commercial airplanes were hijacked and suicidal terrorist attacks were carried out on New York's World Trade Center and the Pentagon headquarters in Washington D.C., killing more than 2,900 people. In the days following the 9/11 attacks, the *New York Times* saw their average daily circulation go up by 130,000 readers, reflecting an increase in the demand for information during times of uncertainty (Josephi, 2004). The importance of scrutinizing bias in journalism has always been an important issue, but in a post-9/11 era, the possibility of bias in reporting Islam-related issues has become a crucial component in media framing.

Nacos and Torres-Reyna (2003) observe that post-9/11, the news coverage of Muslim Americans generated more stories in publications. They state that prior to 9/11, 25% of all sources in the news publications (*New York Times*, *New York Post*, and *New York Daily News*) were identified as Muslim or Arab U.S. citizens or residents versus 41% in the six months following the 9/11 attacks. While it is not unusual that Islam and Muslims became categorized as more newsworthy following the 9/11 attacks, the importance of media depictions of this religion and its followers becomes more pertinent in a world that is fighting the terrorism that may be generated from Islamic countries.

In his book, *Confronting Islamophobia in Educational Practices*, van Driel defines *Islamophobia* as "an irrational distrust, fear or rejection of the Muslim religion and those who are (perceived as) Muslims" (2004, p. x). Haque asserts that Islamophobia is found in the education spectrum of the United States and states "humantics textbooks often carry implicit anti-Islamic messages" (2004, p. 15). Haque (2004) also cites evidence that notable Muslim scholars such as Muhammad al-Khwarizmi (one of the founders of algebra) and Jabir al-Hayyan (who influenced the development of chemistry) are conspicuously absent from American school textbooks. In a post-9/11 world, the influence of these negative frames has the potential to increase racism and misconceptions about Islam and its followers. A democratic government is often times measured by the impartiality and freedom of its press, and there is a critical need to gauge the potential partiality inflicted in the coverage of Islam and Muslims after the 9/11 attacks. Taking into account the post-9/11 influence of international media, along with the increasing Muslim

American population in the United States, further research that thoroughly inspects the correlation between social impact on Muslim Americans and media depictions of their religion is necessary.

The primary purpose of this study is to explore media depictions and framing techniques used in *New York Times'* articles published about Islam and Muslims in the month prior to and following the 9/11 attacks on the World Trade Center and the Pentagon. The secondary purpose of this study is to analyze and compare descriptive text surrounding the words *Islam* and *Muslim* in *New York Times'* articles pre-9/11 and post-9/11. In 1999, the *Columbia Journalism Review* conducted a survey asking 100 leading newspaper editors in the United States to measure the accuracy, integrity, and influence on the broader journalistic community of newspapers in America and the *New York Times* was voted the top newspaper (Vivian, 2005). The *New York Times* was chosen for this study due to its' international reach and elite status for influencing the standard of coverage for other media outlets (e.g. Ashley & Olson, 1998; Haigh et al., 2006; Ross & Bantimaroudis, 2006).

Chapter 2 – Literature Review

This chapter will provide a comprehensive understanding of international media proliferation, the theory of framing, along with varying viewpoints and censorship during times of war. This chapter will also present an overview of the cultivation theory and the history of Arab bias in American media.

Global Media Proliferation and Framing

To better understand the pragmatic relevance of global media in relation to communication, it is necessary to first understand the environment of the media industry. Montgomerie asserts that "because the media of a democratic society functions as a primary means of information access, in order to understand a democratic system, one must understand the media" (2005, p. 5). In the past decade, acquisitions and mergers have resulted in six companies dominating the American mass media market and less than ten dominating the global media market (Ozanich & Wirth, 2004). It is important to note that the publication analyzed for this research, the *New York Times*, is not owned by one of the six media companies referenced above. Bracci asserts that "the widespread proliferation positions media as a cultural industry, producing a set of values and aspirations for consumers to absorb" (2003, p. 126). The current media conglomerates have not formed out of natural *free markets*; they are the result of numerous state policies which have assisted in making media giants formidable political lobbyists at regional, national and global levels (McChesney, 2005).

The apparent flaw in this type of organizational model can be explained by using Bracci's example of the Disney conglomerate, as follows:

> Through merger activities, the Disney movie studio controls the production, storage, distribution, and viewing outlets for all of their affiliated productions. Through movie production in its own studio, Disney also sells video cassettes of its movies and plays them on the Disney cable channel. American Broadcasting Company, a Disney subsidiary, provides a tempting venue to report on and review new Disney productions. This organizational arrangement affords Disney enormous potential power to promulgate a set of values globally to millions of children and their families, with few dissonant voices able to break through. (2003, p. 123)

3

The Disney example helps illustrate that as international media becomes more condensed, global communication also becomes increasingly indistinguishable, self-censoring, and consequential.

Mass media are instrumental tools for communicating information, especially in times of crisis and uncertainty, as was the case for the 9/11 terrorist attacks. Recent studies show that since March 2003, when the invasion of Iraq began, 77% of the people in Iraq have used the television as their main source of information (Smith, 2005). Stempel and Hargrove (2002) establish that post-9/11, 69% of Americans turned to television for information about the terrorist attacks and the war on terrorism. The pragmatic rationale to better examine the *New York Times'* representation of Muslims becomes relevant as global media evolve into homogenous and influential forms of communication.

Reynolds and Barnett (2003) conducted a qualitative study deconstructing Cable News Network's (CNN) audio and video frames of *breaking news* reports of live, unscripted coverage during the first 12 hours after the 9/11 attacks. The researchers' findings suggested that "CNN created a powerful visual and verbal frame with its coverage by arguing to viewers that the events of September 11 comprised an act of war so horrific that immediate military retaliation was not only justified but necessary" (Reynolds & Barnett, 2003, p. 86). Reynolds and Barnett (2003) identified the necessity to examine media communication content by elaborating that it is the starting point for determining media influences and forecasting media effects. The study began by examining 12 hours of video coverage that started at 8:48 a.m. on 9/11/2001, when the first news agency, CNN, broke into a commercial break to report that an explosion had occurred at the World Trade Center in New York City. The videotapes were transcribed and accuracy reviews were conducted prior to any further analysis. Results uncovered three main thematic clusters of judgment, and "CNN's early framing of the events of September 11 created the impression that war was inevitable and necessary to combat the horror and devastation that Americans had just witnessed" (Reynolds & Barnett, 2003, p. 92).

The first main thematic cluster involved war and military response. After receiving confirmation about the terrorist attacks from President George W. Bush at 9:30 a.m. on 9/11/2001, journalists began communicating with symbolic keywords to contextualize the events (Reynolds & Barnett, 2003). Keywords such as *war* were heard 234 times in 12 hours; common descriptions of the terrorists included *cowards* and *madmen*; unconventional references to *God*

4

and the *need to pray* or *prayer* were mentioned 61 times, frequently by journalists (Reynolds & Barnett, 2003).

Often when sources were asked for their opinions about the attacks, many answers were similar to that of Arizona Senator John McCain who stated: "This is obviously an act of war" (Reynolds & Barnett, 2003, p. 93). The study showed that once government sources began mentioning an *act of war*, journalists began assimilating that into the questions they asked. For example, after U.S. Senator Christopher Dodd of Connecticut began comparing the 9/11 attacks to the strike on Pearl Harbor, numerous journalists began directing questions in relation to Pearl Harbor and the idea of a military retaliation started to emerge in media outlets (Reynolds & Barnett, 2003). Reynolds and Barnett (2003) assert that credible evidence was found indicating that numerous government sources were utilizing CNN to communicate messages of international support to other world leaders. From a communication perspective, CNN played an influential role in delivering government-driven propaganda in the hours following the 9/11 attacks.

The second thematic cluster consisted of the substantial attention given to American unity. Reynolds and Barnett (2003) contend that CNN broadcast messages of unity between the two political parties, giving television viewers the indication that any political dissent would be unpatriotic, given the gravity of the terrorist attacks. During the first 12 hours after the attacks, only sources affiliated with the Republican and Democratic parties were interviewed and coinciding, straightforward statements made by the two parties implied that the entire country would be in agreement regarding terrorist-related decisions to come (Reynolds & Barnett, 2003). Reynolds and Barnett substantiate that "one underlying assumption in the choice and language of CNN's official sources and reporters was that Democrats and Republicans made up the entire spectrum of all available viewpoints" (2003, p. 94).

The third thematic cluster issued justification for a U.S. military counter-attack and impressions of patriotic beliefs were used in dialogues to justify a swift response to the terrorist attacks (Reynolds & Barnett, 2003). Justification themes were demonstrated verbally when officials attributed the terrorist attacks with historical context and meaning, as with the Pearl Harbor reference. The strongest example of this came from New York City's Mayor, Rudy Giuliani, who said the attacks were "one of the most heinous acts, certainly in world history" (Reynolds & Barnett, 2003, p. 95). Giuliani's statement supplied historical context while providing credence to the enormity of the attacks. Aside from continuous visual images of the airplanes attacking the towers and aid workers sifting through the rubble, the only out-of-context images shown during the first 12 hours after the attack were that of Palestinian civilians celebrating in East Jerusalem (Reynolds & Barnett, 2003). These visuals were in direct contrast to the images of the attacks and recovery efforts under way. CNN aired that clip three times between 3:35 p.m. and 3:45 p.m. and "their juxtaposition with the images of the death and destruction in the United States were further examples of ways that seemingly disconnected video could reinforce the general themes offered in the audio, creating strong arousal within viewers" (Reynolds & Barnett, 2003, p. 100).

Through the three thematic clusters, it becomes evident that content on CNN dominated American ideologies and comments made by journalists showed more commentary and interpretation and less journalistic objectivity. Reynolds and Barnett's (2003) study found evidence that CNN's breaking news coverage of 9/11 created a powerful visual and verbal frame and communicated to viewers that the attacks were the beginning of a war in which the United States needed to respond to swiftly with military reprisal. This coincides with McChesney's idea that "crucial political issues are warped to fit the confines of an elite debate, stripping ordinary citizens of the toll they need to be informed, active participants in a democracy" (2000, p. 281).

The Theory of Framing

Entman states that "to frame is to select some aspects of a perceived reality and make them more salient in a communicating text, in such a way as to promote a particular problem, definition, causal interpretation, moral evaluation, and/or treatment recommendation for the item described" (1993, p. 52). Tankard, Hendrickson, Silberman, Bliss and Ghanem define a media frame as "the central organizing idea for news content that supplies a context and suggests what the issue is through the use of selection, emphasis, exclusion and elaboration" (1991, p. 3). Framing can be a significant tool in measuring the bias and power of media in society. The way in which journalists frame issues can have a deep impact on the way readers perceive that information (Entman, 1993).

Norris, Kern, and Just further explain that "the essence of framing is selection to prioritize some facts, images, or developments over others, thereby unconsciously promoting one particular interpretation of events" (2003, p.11). Gitlin asserts that "frames enable journalists to

6

process large amounts of information quickly and routinely: to recognize it as information, to assign it to cognitive categories, and to package it for efficient relay to their audiences" (1980, p. 7). Agenda-setting, as famously conceptualized by Bernard Cohen, concentrates on the fact that "the press may not be successful much of the time in telling *people* [italics added] what to think about, but it is stunningly successful in telling its *readers* [italics added] what to think about….The world will look different to different people, depending….on the map that is drawn for them by writers, editors, and publishers of the paper they read" (1963, p. 13). Recently, some researchers have classified the theory of framing as second level agenda-setting, and McCombs, Shaw and Weaver (1997) argue that framing and agenda-setting are converged where framing can be seen as an extension of agenda-setting. Maslog, Lee, and Kim assert that "object salience is transmitted in the first level of agenda-setting process. In the second level, framing, viewed as indicator salience, illustrates that the media tell us *how* [italics added] to think about something" (2006, p. 24-25).

While conducting a study on the impact of story selection on framing, Gans (1979) came up with the following nine theories pertaining to story selection:

1. Journalist-centered: the coverage is influenced by the professional news judgment of the journalist.
2. Organization-centered: the coverage is influenced by the commercial or business focus of the organization.
3. Event-centered: The event determines what makes the news.
4. Technological theory: the story selection is determined by the technology of the communication channel.
5. Economic theory: National economy will determine the coverage.
6. Marxism: In monopoly capitalism, journalists become the public relations mediator.
7. Cultural theory: Story selection is decided by the values of the national culture.
8. Audience-centered: The coverage is determined by what the people want.
9. Source-centered: The news is influenced by journalists' sources.

In the first ever systematic national poll of its kind, the *American Muslim Poll* was executed by Georgetown University's Project MAPS in October and November of 2001 to delve into the beliefs about Muslim Americans (Nacos & Torres-Reyna, 2003). Results indicated that more than two in three (68%) respondents believed that, in general, American news media outlets were unfair and biased in their portrayal of Muslims and Islam (Nacos & Torres-Reyna, 2003). Nacos and Torres-Reyna expand on this topic by giving an example shortly after 9/11 when "some Arab merchants in Brooklyn tried to organize a boycott of the *New York Post* to dramatize their opposition to what they believed was an anti-Arab and anti-Muslim stance" and passed out flyers stating that the *New York Post* "is not only pro-Zionist, but it hates everything called Islamic or Arabic" (2003, p. 134).

Nacos and Torres-Reyna (2003) conducted a study to see whether American news media used negative and stereotypical frames toward Muslim Americans post-9/11. The researchers compared news coverage of Muslim and Arab Americans pre- and post-9/11 through the analysis of four newspapers: *New York Times*, *New York Post*, *USA Today*, and *New York Daily News*. Nacos and Torres-Reyna anticipated heavy coverage of Muslim American news stories following 9/11 and therefore limited their time periods for analysis to 12 months prior to the attacks and six months following the 9/11 attacks. The researchers reported on the placement of articles, the type of news (editorial, reporting, etc.) and the geographical context of the stories. Altogether, 867 articles were analyzed from the four publications listed above.

As expected, results showed that there was a significant increase in the number of articles about Muslim Americans post-9/11; however, the researchers were surprised to learn that the four newspapers combined published almost eleven times as many such news items in the six months following the 9/11 attacks, as compared to six months prior to the attacks (Nacos & Torres-Reyna, 2003). Another interesting point revealed in the research was the amount of coverage that the *New York Post* and *New York Daily News* gave to Muslim American campaign contributions made to Hillary Clinton in her campaign for the New York senate seat. Nacos and Torres-Reyna elaborate how the *New York Post* persistently charged Clinton with allegedly having ties to terrorist-friendly groups. Typical quotes in news articles and editorials included "Do you believe that Israel has a right to exist? Do you believe that America needs a dependable, democratically in the strategically vital, oil-rich Middle East? Then Hillary's record should really give you pause" (2003, p. 143). In the end, Hillary Clinton returned the campaign contributions.

Other results showed that the private lives of Muslim Americans were given much less media attention after the 9/11 attacks, whereas prior to 9/11, 14% of all stories about Muslim Americans concerned stories about private life (Nacos & Torres-Reyna, 2003). In the aftermath of the 9/11 attacks, the most-covered topics regarding Muslim and Arab American citizens and residents concerned their civil liberties, civil rights, and immigration issues--an increase from 6% to 30% (Nacos & Torres-Reyna, 2003). It is interesting to note the fact that Nacos and Torres-Reyna found depictions of Muslim Americans to be more positive after the 9/11 attacks and three of the newspapers studied (*New York Times, New York Post, USA Today*) portrayed Muslim and Arab Americans more favorably than unfavorably post-9/11 (Nacos & Torres-Reyna, 2003).

The fourth newspaper studied, the *New York Daily News*, was found to carry an equal portion of positive and negative articles about Muslim Americans, after the 9/11 attacks (Nacos & Torres-Reyna, 2003). The biggest shift found was related to episodic and thematic stories after 9/11 where news stories in the four publications were less episodic and more thematic. The researchers found this to be an improvement and explained the significance of thematic stories (versus episodic): "When stories provide readers with more than bare-bone facts and explain news events in a larger context, news consumers get more comprehensive information and are able to make their evaluation of individuals and groups on a more informed and educated basis" (Nacos & Torres-Reyna, 2003, p. 151). Nacos and Torres-Reyna (2003) concluded that their research found a shift from fairly limited and stereotypical news presentations before the 9/11 attacks to more thorough and contemplative news coverage in the aftermath of 9/11. Reporters covered Muslim Americans more frequently in news stories and cited them more regularly as sources for information following the attacks (Nacos & Torres-Reyna, 2003).

In another study, Maslog, Lee, and Kim (2006) conducted a content analysis that examined the way Asian news outlets framed the coverage of the Iraq war. The researchers employed the news frames of war journalism and peace journalism to measure dominant frames used by newspapers and news agencies in the five Asian countries of India, Pakistan, Philippines, Sri Lanka, and Indonesia. War journalism is generally "characterized by an identification with one or the home side of the conflict, military triumphanist language, an action-oriented focus, and a superficial narrative with little context, background or historical perspective" with the focus on winning the war (Maslog, Lee, & Kim, 2006, p. 20). The researchers define peace journalism as "an advocacy, interpretative approach that highlights peace initiatives; tones down ethnic and religious differences; prevents further conflict; focuses on the structure of society; and promotes conflict resolution, reconstruction and reconciliation" (Maslog, Lee, & Kim, 2006, p. 20).

9

Maslog, Lee, and Kim (2006) analyzed 422 stories from seven English-language Asian daily newspapers and the majority of them (289 or 65.4%) were *hard* news. *Hard* news deals with official or serious news, such as in a newspaper or television report, whereas *soft* news deals with not-so-serious topics, such as infotainment (The American Heritage Dictionary of the English Language, n.d.). The two key components of *hard* news are seriousness (topics such as politics, economics, crime, war, and disasters) and timeliness (coverage of current events).

Results of all the articles combined showed that the majority of the news stories (50.7%) were framed as peace journalism. Another 44.1% of the news stories were framed as war journalism and 5.2% were determined to be neutral (Maslog, Lee, & Kim, 2006). However, when researchers examined each country individually, significant disparity was found. News media from the predominantly Muslim countries of Pakistan and Indonesia used war journalism frames less frequently than the non-Muslim countries of India and Sri Lanka, with the exception of the Philippines (Maslog, Lee, & Kim, 2006). The strongest peace journalism frames were found in the Indonesian, Pakistani, and Philippines' newspapers. A significant relationship was found between the support for the Iraq war and whether a story was picked up from the foreign wires or produced locally. Research indicated that locally-produced stories were strongly (18.6%) or moderately (13.6%) anti-war compared to foreign wire stories which found 9.6% that were strongly anti-war and 5.6% that were moderately anti-war (Maslog, Lee, & Kim, 2006).

The findings also demonstrated that newspapers from non-Muslim countries were significantly more supportive of the Americans/British whereas Muslim countries were significantly more supportive of the Iraqis (Maslog, Lee, & Kim, 2006). The researchers concluded: "In attempting to understand how a conflict is covered, framed and interpreted by news media from other countries that are not involved in the conflict, this study found that religion and sourcing are two important factors shaping the framing of Asian news coverage on the Iraq war" (Maslog, Lee, & Kim, 2006, p. 32).

In another study regarding print media framing, Ashley and Olson (1998) conducted analysis of the women's movement from 1966 to 1986. The works of Gitlin (2003) along with Gamson and Modigliani (1989) assert that media frames are employed through the principles of selection, exclusion, emphasis and presentation while remaining characteristically unnoticed by the receiver of the media content. Ashley and Olson (1998) conducted content and descriptive analyses on the *New York Times*, *Time Magazine*, and *Newsweek* to determine which framing techniques were employed by news print media in the coverage of the women's movement.

Ashley and Olson (1998) coded framing using the following four categories:

1. Importance, defined by the amount of coverage each word received, story topic, and section placement of articles (Shoemaker, 1984).
2. Illegitimacy, where quotation marks were used to trivialize movement, appearance of protesters was discussed, protesters were undercounted, and internal dissension was emphasized (Gitlin, 2003).
3. Deviance, when the stories emphasized violence (Gitlin, 2003).
4. Event coverage, defined by focus on the actual event rather than the group's issues (Staggenborg, 1993).

The researchers used the works of Gitlin (2003), Paletz and Entman (1981), Pan and Kosickiby (1993), and Parenti (1986) to conclude that "news media can frame a protest group in several ways: by ignoring it; burying the article in the back section; by the description given to the protesters; reporting the events rather than the group's goals and interests; trivializing the protest by making light of their dress, language, age, style, or goals; or marginalizing viewpoints by attributing them to a social deviant" (Ashley & Olson, 1998, p. 264). Results uncovered that the women's movement was indeed marginalized by the press, and the majority of coverage analyzed rarely included the organization's goals, focusing more heavily on deviant behavior (Ashley & Olson, 1998).

Varying Viewpoints and Censorship in Times of War

The reporting of news stories in the aftermath of 9/11 demonstrated significant disparity on international and American perceptions of the wars on Afghanistan and Iraq. Iskandar (2005) illustrates the polarization of public opinion by pointing out that international media outlets' continuously reported that the American public was being exposed to drastically contrasting coverage of the Iraq war in comparison to the rest of the world.

Gallup International (2003) conducted two international polls between January and May 2003, in conjunction with the Pew Research Center (PRC). The PRC conducted one international poll in April-May 2003 with the intention of measuring global support and opposition for the war in Iraq. Fifty-six countries were surveyed in three polls (including 20 European countries); and results indicated that, with the exception of the United States, every single country's majority refuted one-sided military action in Iraq (Gallup International, 2003). The research also found that countries which were polled on the subject of military involvement (38 countries polled on this topic, 20 from Europe) had an 89% majority that opposed the possibility of their government providing military assistance in Iraq (Gallup International, 2003). Yet, in a survey conducted by the Program on International Policy Attitudes (PIPA) and Knowledge Networks (2003), 56% of all people surveyed in the United States (from June to September 2003) believed that international public opinion was supportive of the war and occupation in Iraq. In the same survey conducted by PIPA and Knowledge Networks (2003), 57% of the participants in America believed that Iraq had provided some support for Al-Qaeda, with 22% in that population believing that Iraq had been directly involved in carrying out the 9/11 attacks.

Along with this disparity of opinions and facts regarding the wars in Afghanistan and Iraq, an inadvertent reaction came from the international audience who regarded the American government's war propaganda campaign unfavorably. A Pew Center survey conducted in the months following the start of the Iraqi war showed that the ratings of America's image had drastically decreased internationally (Iskandar, 2005). In France and Great Britain, there was a significant 31% decrease in American favorability, Russia showed a 28% decrease, and there was a 25% decrease in German approval ratings towards American actions (Iskandar, 2005).

The Bush administration's claim that terrorists attacked America because of its' symbolic representations of freedom and democracy may have assisted in increasing levels of patriotism among Americans (Brewer, Aday, & Gross, 2003). Brewer, Aday, and Gross (2003) conducted a two-wave national random digit-dial telephone survey of Americans over the age of eighteen. Data was collected for the first wave from the period of October 24th until November 5th of 2001, while the second wave took place from February 28th to March 26th, 2002. Results indicated that symbolic patriotism had a considerable positive effect on presidential support, and the researchers summarize that "citizens who rallied around the flag also rallied around the president. Thus, our results provide evidence for a causal mechanism underlying presidential approval during times of crisis" (Brewer, Aday, & Gross, 2003, p. 243). The researchers further elaborate that since presidential views of issues were more prominent in the aftermath of 9/11, "presidential support lifted confidence in institutions under presidential authority – namely, the military and intelligence agencies – and even another branch of government, Congress" (2003, p. 247).

Another trait that became prominent in the patriotic, post-9/11 world of journalism was that of self-censorship. Mark Jurkowitz, a reporter for the *Boston Globe*, cited anecdotal evidence six months after the 9/11 attacks, and discussed how reporters decreased their anti-war criticism editorial comments because of fear of being labeled unpatriotic by fellow press members (Hess & Kalb, 2003). Robert Siegel, the anchor for National Public Radio's *All Things Considered,* asserted that even though historically journalists had been the ones to produce the *first draft of history*, in the aftermath of the 9/11 attacks, news correspondents saw the Pentagon, and, more specifically, Defense Secretary Donald Rumsfeld, giving daily briefs and controlling all messages in the public relations realm at the time (Hess & Kalb, 2003).

Norris, Kern, and Just (2003) maintain that, in wartime, governments obtain justifiable control over press coverage. CNN journalist Christiane Amanpour stated in an interview that her network was among one of many that had "self-muzzled" and that her news network "was intimidated by the administration and its foot soldiers at Fox News" (Iskandar, 2005, p. 169). Amanpour explained that problems in covering the war on Iraq focused on the way that stories were framed and the avoidance of asking crucial questions, indicating that disinformation was being delivered from the highest levels of government (Iskandar, 2005).

The extensive framing affected news media sources such that they joined in compliance with the agendas set by the Bush administration. Jensen explains that "since 9/11, it has been painfully clear that the mainstream commercial news media have not been, on the whole, that much-needed critical, independent voice and are far from neutral sources of information" (2005, p. 68). Iskandar (2005) points out the *Fox Effect* in which cable news networks followed the lead of Republican-leaning Fox News Channel and adapted more conservative and biased ways to report news coverage. She asserts that MSNBC (a combination of the Microsoft Network and the National Broadcasting Company) discontinued the liberal-leaning talk show *Donahue* a month before the war in Iraq started and replaced it with "a slew of ideologues who espouse reactionary conservative positions" (2005, p. 168).

Cultivation Theory and Newspapers

The premise of the cultivation theory is that the more exposure a person has to television, the more likely their idea of reality will duplicate that of the mass-mediated messages seen on television. Cultivation analysis studies the contribution television makes to viewers' perceptions of social reality and focuses on the comparison and outcomes of cumulative exposure to television over extended periods of time (Gerber & Gross, 1976). Gerbner and Gross (1976) argue that 'heavy' viewers of television would be more influenced by the power of media, altering their perception of reality over time, whereas 'light' viewers of television would be less affected. Cultivation is also a theory of social control as it "examines how media are used in social systems to build consensus (if not agreement) on positions through shared terms of discourse and assumptions about priorities and values" (Shanahan & Morgan, 1999, p. 15).

The need to examine the influential abilities of television was developed from the Cultural Indicators research program at the University of Pennsylvania in the 1960's. The Cultural Indicators project was formed when the National Commission on the Causes and Prevention of Violence funded a content analysis study of violence in prime-time programming during the 1967-68 television season (Gerbner & Gross, 1976). George Gerbner was the lead on this research project at the University of Pennsylvania's Annenberg School of Communication and initiated the first phase of the Cultural Indicators Project which ultimately "documented the frequency and nature of television violence and established a baseline for long-term monitoring of the world of television" (Shanahan & Morgan, 1999, p.7). Gerbner created the basis of cultural indicators as a way to effectively measure important cultural issues in society. The Cultural Indicators research concentrated on the prevalent use of television and its consequences because the research team believed that television had become America's collective dispenser of shared cultural values and social realities. The concept of cultural indicators was a milestone in mass communication research because it asserted that television's precise message patterns reflected underlying cultural values (Shanahan, 2004).

The research project was constructed as a three-part structure for investigating the basis and consequences of the ubiquitous cultural symbols. Shanahan and Morgan (1999) best summarize the three prongs as:

1. The process, pressure and limitations that affect the production of mass-mediated messages.

2. The prevailing, cumulative patterns of visual and verbal messages, values, information, and teachings articulated through mass media content.
3. The relationship between the impact of this content and a viewer's conception of social reality.

All three prongs involve unique framework and methodologies starting with the first prong, *institutional process analysis* which is employed to investigate how mass-mediated messages are chosen, produced, and distributed (Shanahan & Morgan, 1999). The second prong, *message system analysis* is used to quantify and track "patterns of demography, action structures, relationships, aspects of life and recurrent images in media content, in terms of the portrayal of violence, minorities, gender-roles, occupations" (Shanahan & Morgan, 1999, p. 7). The third prong of *media effects* concerns cultivation analysis where the relationship between mass-mediated messages and their correlation to viewer perceptions of social reality is studied (Shanahan & Morgan, 1999).

Though the Cultural Indicators project was significant in many ways, the research that emerged on cultivation theory quickly overshadowed the impact of cultural indicators (Shanahan & Morgan, 1999). The development of the cultivation theory "emerged from a historical period in which the prevailing intellectual view was that media had at most only minimal effects, that any effects were likely only to echo pre-existing dispositions" (Shanahan & Morgan, 1999, p. 11). Fisher (1984) asserts that the majority of message-effects research had traditionally indicated that human communication was made up of an exchange of information while cultivation perceived human communication to be story-telling transactions. Historically, stories were told face-to-face by community members such as parents, teachers, and religious leaders in order to preserve and grow cultural values. The emergence of television in society dramatically altered this system. Television became the most frequently-used medium and Berger stresses that "as our primary storyteller, it cultivates or reinforces certain values and beliefs in its viewers" (1995, p. 66).

A key component of cultivation is that of cultivation analysis which focuses on the *effects* segment of Gerbner's three-prong theory. Shanahan and Morgan affirm that "prior to the development of cultivation analysis, then, most researchers in mass communication were interested in knowing how specific messages, channels and sources could produce changes in attitudes or behaviors" (1999, p. 9). Even though the cultivation theory was originally formed as a theory of social control, cultivation analysis quickly became the focal point because during that time, the effects of violence on television was starting to become a major social concern. Gandy (1999) made an interesting assertion that many scholars focused on cultivation analysis and the *effects* of television instead of the *systems and institutions* prong of Gerbner's theory because early fund contributors such as the Rockefeller Foundation wanted the focus on media directed away from the critical study of the structures of ownership and control.

Traditionally, the cultivation theory has been employed to assess the effects of television but as the theory has progressed, so has the realm of focus. Vergeer, Lubbers, and Scheepers (2000) conducted an innovative study to measure whether newspapers in the Netherlands were cultivating negative attitudes toward ethnic minorities. The study focused on readers' perception of ethnic issues in correlation with ethnic stories that ran in three of the most prominent and well-distributed newspapers in the Netherlands, the *Volkskrant*, the *Gelderlander*, and the *Telegraaf*. The *Volkskrant* holds the country's third-largest market share and is generally viewed as a progressive newspaper whereas the *Telegraaf* is a conservative publication and holds the largest market share. The *Gelderlander* is the Netherlands' largest regional newspaper publication. The researchers wanted to gauge whether exposure to newspaper articles about ethnic minorities would be related to adverse attitudes in readers' perceptions of ethnic minorities.

Data was collected from the Netherlands using five random surveys between 1990 and 1995 using a stratified sample to measure if participants perceived ethnic minorities as more threatening. The three items used for the demographic measures were level of education, distribution of housing, and cutbacks on social security. The researchers used multiple regression analysis to determine the strength of the relationship between exposure to newspapers and attitudes toward ethnic minorities.

The researchers explain that exposure to different newspapers have different effects on readers' perception of ethnic threat; some newspapers focus more attention on ethnic minorities and some may highlight the pejorative aspects of these ethnic minorities more strongly than other newspapers (Vergeer, Lubbers, & Scheepers, 2000). Content analysis uncovered that the *Telegraaf* published more articles about ethnic crime than the *Volkskrant* and the *Gelderlander*. Vergeer, Lubbers, and Scheepers (2000) even cite previous studies conducted on these three newspapers that showed the *Telegraaf* associated ethnic minorities with menacing aspects such as crime whereas the *Volkskrant* associated ethnic minorities less frequently with threatening features.

Results indicated that people who were exposed to the *Telegraaf* viewed ethnic minorities as more threatening than those people who read the *Volkskrant*. The perceived threat wasn't significantly different between people that read the *Telegraaf* and the *Gelderlander*. With the exception of *Telegraaf* and *Gelderlander*, people that were exposed to more than one newspaper perceived ethnic minorities as less threatening. Participants who had received less education perceived ethnic minorities as more of a threat than participants who had a university degree. The participants who had received an average level of education perceived ethnic minorities as more threatening than college-educated participants but not as threatening as the least-educated participants. Average level of education, as defined by the researchers, was the completion of A-levels and O-levels, roughly equivalent to the completion of high school in America (Vergeer, Lubbers, & Scheepers, 2000).

Results also indicated that participants older than 60 years of age perceived ethnic minorities as more threatening than young participants that were between the ages of 18 and 24. People who voted for right-wing political parties also viewed ethnic minorities as more threatening than the participants who voted for left-wing or religious parties. This study was innovative because Vergeer, Lubbers, and Scheepers elaborated the "cultivation theory by applying it to attitudes toward ethnic minorities," and designated the newspaper, rather than television, as the transporter of messages (2000, p. 139). The research concluded with the suggestion that future research should focus on the cumulative effects of being exposed to multiple mass media.

History of Arab Bias in American Media

Though 15 million of the 265 million Arabs are Christians, popular belief associates Arabs with Islam and the Muslim world (Shaheen, 2001). The population of Muslim Americans is estimated to range from three to six million people in the United States with more than half of this population earning an income of at least $50,000 a year and 58% having college degrees (Haque, 2004). Shaheen maintains that "new reports selectively and relentlessly focus on a minority of a minority of Arabs, the radical fringe. The seemingly indelible Arab-as-villain image wrongly conveys the message that the vast majority of the 265 million peace-loving Arabs

17

are bad guys" (2001, p. 28). The examination of the history of Arabs in American media is necessary in order to further assess frames used for Arab depiction.

In his book *Reel Bad Arabs*, Jack Shaheen (2001) explores Arab stereotypes utilized in Hollywood films. Shaheen (2001) asserts that the importance of scrutinizing this matter lies in the international influence propagated by the Hollywood motion picture industry and that stereotypical Arab images not only provoke international audiences, but international film makers as well. Along with cataloging more than 900 films that depict Muslim Arabs in a negative manner, Shaheen (2001) also considers the rationale behind such practices by hypothesizing that this is partly due to news reports that focus heavily on the marginal group of Arabs that are fanatics. Shaheen (2001) alleges that the popular image of Arabs as religious zealots began in the 1940's which saw the conflict of Israel and Palestine lead to the wars of 1948, 1967, and 1973, along with the Iranian hostage crisis in the 1980's and the Gulf War of the 1990's. Another explanation put forth by film critic Anthony Lane is that it is easy to replace any ethnic group with Arabs at this point in time and claims: "So, here's a party game for any producers with a Middle Eastern setting in mind; try replacing one Semitic group with another-- Jew instead of Arabs--and THEN listen for laughs" (as cited in Shaheen, 2001, p. 9).

In his extensive study, Shaheen found more than 900 feature films that depicted Arabs as villains and the majority of them were "sheikhs, maidens, Egyptians, and Palestinians" whereas the remainder were "devious dark-complexioned baddies from other Arab countries such as Algerians, Iraqis, Jordanians, Lebanese, Libyans, Moroccans, Syrians, Tunisians, and Yemeni" (2001, p.13). Shaheen (2001) maintains that exposure to such images may have strong impact on young viewers, who may duplicate the cinematic stereotypes to which they are exposed.

Another sphere where Arab bias may be found is in the educational practices of the United States. Sheridan (2004) asserts that Muslim students in American higher education establishments have found apparent religious discrimination and bias to be a common facet of their educational experience. Sheridan (2004) elaborates on how research has shown that discriminatory attitudes can be influenced through educational experiences in the following three ways: First, educational institutions can directly impact religious, racial, ethnic, and cultural association. Second, young people are affected by positive and negative attitudes of professors and teachers. Third, the education curriculum can covertly or directly propagate or challenge stereotypes, leading to promotion or reflection of prejudicial attitudes. Sheridan (2004)

18

concludes that the effects of Arab bias in educational settings may be just as influential as those found in Hollywood motion pictures and, in some instances, harder to distinguish.

Richardson (2004) conducted a study of elite British broadsheet newspapers that illustrate how journalists consistently produced anti-Muslim sentiments in their writings. Richardson (2004) argues that journalists use argumentative strategies in their writing in order to make their version of the reported action appear credible, then at the same time, distance themselves from these very claims, so as to appear reasonable and legitimate, in order to maintain the impression of objectivity. Richardson asserts that "journalism is a genre in which journalists attempt to promote the acceptance of their arguments in the eyes of the audience and hence persuade this audience of the adequacy of their point of view" (2004, p. 228). Though this study was conducted in England, its applicability to the international spectrum is valid because "given the centripetal forces of political and economic globalization, the greater standardization of journalistic texts and the widespread and continuing influence of Orientalist scholarship (particularly in the 'West'), the conclusions offered may be useful to studies of broadsheet, or 'quality' newspaper reporting in other countries" (Richardson, 2004, p. xvi).

Richardson's study found that the British broadsheet journalists divided and rejected Muslims in the newspapers through a three-part process: they first identified a *space* which could be social, physical or mental, and rhetorically separated it from their *own space*; then they explained the workings or compositions of the space in contrast to their own space, and finally the newspapers placed a negative social value on the space and composition (Richardson, 2004). Richardson explains that these three processes of separation, differentiation and negativization were used to depict Muslims in a negative light and used notions of "civility, modernity, a linear and universal notion of 'social progress'; and the inferior position of the identified 'Muslim space' in comparison to ours" (2004, p. 232).

Carol Natanson-Moog states that "the relentless stress of people grinning and pouting and dancing and slinking and munching and exhorting out at us from radios, billboards, magazines, and TV screens aren't just selling toothpaste--they are selling identities" (as cited in Yumul, 2004, p. 35). Yumul asserts that "the apparatuses of discourse play a critical role not only in fostering our sense of collective identity, but also in establishing who are to be included and who are to be excluded from the very definition of collectivity by elucidating the content of the collective identity, or at least by verifying its sociocultural validity" (2004, p. 35).

19

Yumul (2004) employs the use of an example from a Turkish advertisement to illustrate how ethnic stereotypes trickle into commercials and provoke similar beliefs in the viewers. In a commercial for Audi cars, a man's shirtless, hairy body is seen (whose face is cut out from the screenshots) wearing a noticeable gold medallion and carrying a rosary. A visible slogan can be seen on the screen that reads: "the accessories that you can never find at Audi" (Yumul, 2004, p. 43). Yumul assesses that "the accessories are used as signifiers of the inner qualities and attributes of a group of people who came to be designated as 'black Turks' in Turkey in order to demarcate them from 'white' or 'Euro' Turks" (2004, p. 43). Yumul (2004) explains the distinction between the 'white' and 'black' Turks as that of those people who have gone through the civilizing process and those who have not. It is further elaborated that 'white' Turks are those considered to be urban, middle- or upper-class educated, having adopted Western lifestyles, and being of fair complexion and physically attractive. On the other hand, the commercial employs the use of 'black' Turks that represents Eastern origins, and, as a result, illustrates countrified and uneducated inclinations (Yumul, 2004).

Another example regarding the bias seen in American media can be seen using the case of the Arab news network Al-Jazeera. The Al-Jazeera news network is based in Qatar, a tiny country about the size of an average-size U.S. city, with 744,500 people by 2000 estimates (El-Nawawy & Iskandar, 2003). Funding for the news network comes primarily from Qatar's progressive, Western-educated monarch, Sheikh Hamad bin Khalifa Al-Thani (El-Nawawy & Iskandar, 2003). El-Nawawy and Iskandar note the following:

> Al-Jazeera is a textbook example of what media scholars Joseph Staubhaar and Marwan Kraidy call asymmetrical interdependence. As millions of Arab satellite subscribers throughout the Middle East, North America, and Europe tune in to watch Al-Jazeera, it could be convincingly argued that the network's influence and impact on international affairs and public opinion is disproportionate to the miniscule amount of power that the Qatari state exerts politically. (2003, p. 32)

With an estimated 35 million viewers worldwide, Al-Jazeera has substantial viewership in the United States (El-Nawawy & Iskandar, 2003). The Arab-American population alone is estimated between three to six million in the United States and a significant portion of them have watched Al-Jazeera at one point or another (Sheler & Betzold, 2001). Somewhat contrary to the network's increasing popularity with viewers, the United States government has been suspicious

20

of Al-Jazeera and publicly accused the channel of being a mouthpiece for terrorists and other American enemies (La Guardia & Skidels, 2005). In particular, there is a very apparent clash between the current American government's views, especially those espoused by the Republican administration, and Arab communities in the United States who find Al-Jazeera programming to be more accurate than Western network news (El-Nawawy & Iskandar, 2003).

Considerable evidence has been documented to suggest that Al-Jazeera has been systematically targeted by the Bush Administration post-9/11. Parenti elaborates that "so far the American military has bombed the network's offices in both Baghdad and Kabul, killing one employee; arrested and briefly jailed 21 of Al-Jazeera's reporters; and now has imprisoned and allegedly abused and humiliated [reporters] Hassan and Darwish in ways that the U.N. convention on such matters would consider torture" (2004, p. 2).

When the United States organized a regional meeting for Arab nations in the summer of 2004 to discuss political and social initiatives, the United States government declined to invite the state of Qatar because it hosts Al-Jazeera (Hilsum, 2004). One diplomat in attendance asserted that "it's strange having a summit declaration on democratic reforms and not inviting a country because it has a free press" (Hilsum, 2004, p. 10).

MSNBC made controversial headlines in November 2004 when discriminatory remarks were made on the *Imus in the Morning* show ("MSNBC apology not enough," 2004). Commenting on an execution of a wounded Iraqi in Fallujah by an American Marine, a fictitious Senior Military Affairs Advisor excused the killing by referencing a "booby-trapped raghead cadaver. The fictitious advisor also said that killing provided an *Al-Jazeera moment* causing the Muslim masses to respond with their routine packs of rabid sheep mentality" ("MSNBC apology not enough," 2004, p. 4).

Al-Jazeera has come under attack by the Bush administration for being too informative at times and practicing their newfound freedom of speech too enthusiastically. Secretary of State Colin Powell urged the government of Qatar to "tone down" Al-Jazeera's allegedly "inflammatory rhetoric" (Davidson, 2003, p. 172). The Bush administration has attempted to persuade the censorship of Al-Jazeera by initiating involvement of the Qatari government. The Emir of Qatar stated that Bush administration had requested he "exert his influence over Al-Jazeera television station because of its airing of anti-American sentiments" ("U.S. seeks to curb Al-Jazeera's freedom of speech," 2001, p. 9). Secretary of State Condoleezza Rice and other

Bush administration officials appealed to Americans' sense of patriotism and security concerns by persuading news networks to self-censor and not air Al-Jazeera news segments (Schechter, 2004). Al-Jazeera spokesman Jihad Ali Ballout concurred that the Arab news network had been trying to combat censorship pressures since the inception of the broadcast in 1996 (Hanley, 2003).

When the Iraq war began, media networks communicated the Pentagon slogan of *shock and awe* as a boastful military spectacle (Kellner, 2004). It is crucial to point out that "Western audiences experienced this bombing positively as a powerful assault on evil" but Al-Jazeera's live coverage communicated "an attack on the body of the Arab and Muslim people, just as September 11 terror attacks were experienced by Americans as assaults on the very body and symbols of the United States" (Kellner, 2004, p. 71).

With so much evidence indicating that government and media networks employ the extensive use of frames to disseminate information, it is imperative to investigate which frames have been applied to the words *Islam* and *Muslim*. Furthermore, it is important to distinguish whether the frames used prior to the 9/11 attacks changed after the attacks had occurred.

Research Question

RQ1: How were descriptive texts in relation to the keywords *Muslim* and *Islam* framed in *New York Times'* articles following the attacks on 9/11/2001, as compared to the coverage before the attacks occurred?

Chapter 3 – Methodology

Keywords

The investigation included qualitative and quantitative content analyses with framing used as the primary theory. Online search engines LexisNexis Academic, EBSCO Host (Elton B. Stephens Company), Proquest and Info Trac were utilized to collect all relevant articles from the *New York Times*' that used the designated keywords *Islam* and *Muslim* for the 30-day period before and after the 9/11 attacks.

Tables of content, text that accompanied graphics, classified ads, geographic locations, public ads, and people's names that included the words *Islam* and *Muslim* (i.e. Islamabad, Pakistan; President Islam Karimov of Uzbekistan) were discarded from analysis. The words *Islamic*, *Islamophobia* and *Muslims* were included in the analysis.

Initially this research had included the following keywords to be analyzed: *Pakistani, Taliban, extremist, Saudi, Palestinian, Arab, Middle Eastern,* and *terrorist*. However, based on the number of articles found for the post-9/11 data sets, through the use of the online search engine LexisNexis Academic, the keywords were reduced to include only *Islam* and *Muslim*.

Keyword	Pre-9/11	Post-9/11
Pakistani	11	139
Taliban	32	426
Extremist	28	106
Saudi	30	257
Palestinian	198	254
Arab	104	444
Middle Eastern	13	119
Terrorist	81	1000+

Sample

Preliminary searches using LexisNexis Academic yielded 115 articles (08/10/01 – 09/10/01) for *Islam* and 138 articles (08/10/01 – 09/10/01) for *Muslim* for the 30-days leading up to the 9/11 attacks. The 30-days following the attacks generated 693 articles (09/12/01-10/12/01) containing the word *Muslim* and 625 articles (09/12/01-10/12/01) for *Islam*. The number of articles found through this initial search made it sufficient to establish a reliable timeframe for the two months surrounding the attacks. News events that occurred in the 30-days following the 9/11 attacks may have affected the ebb and flow of the number of articles generated for analysis (Appendix A).

Due to the sheer volume of articles found, systematic random sampling was used to retain the quality of data while reducing the number of articles analyzed. Using articles from every third day in the month preceding the 9/11 attacks, 40 articles were found for *Islam* and 47 articles for *Muslim*. Using articles from every fourth day in the month following the 9/11 attacks, 139 articles were found for *Islam* and 160 articles for *Muslim*. That brought the total number of articles analyzed to 386, with 87 articles in the pre-9/11 data set and 299 articles in the post-9/11 data set.

Analysis

The text analysis software, MonoConc Pro 2.2, was used to analyze the context in which the words *Islam* and *Muslim* were used before and after the 9/11 attacks. MonoConc Pro 2.2 is a concordance software that allows users to distinguish formal patterns in text files. Concordance, in its simplest form, can be described as 'text-searching', while a concordancer is a basic program that allows users to search large text files for a word or phrase (Barlow, 2003). News stories, editorials and letters-to-the-editor were utilized as the units of analysis. Analysis of articles in this research excluded the following words, as found in the two words before and two words after the keywords: *a, of, to, in, that, and, that, is, with, on, the, an, if, or, by, as, no, my, it, at, have, he, we, you, who,* and *from*.

24

Chapter 4 – Results

This chapter will examine the findings of the qualitative and quantitative content analysis as it pertains to the research question of how descriptive texts surrounding the keywords *Islam* and *Muslim* were framed in *New York Times'* articles before and after the 9/11 attacks. For more comprehensive details on the analysis, see Tables 1-4 in this chapter and Appendices B-M.

Pre-9/11 Islam Data

Forty articles were analyzed that contained the keyword *Islam* before the 9/11 attacks occurred and the word *Islam* was found 57 times in these articles. The corpus frequency list indicated the most repeatedly-used words, as tallied in each data set. This list assisted in revealing the most recurring contexts in which the articles were placed. The most frequently-mentioned words (aside from the keyword) in these articles were *Israeli*, *Palestinian*, *Israel*, and *Jerusalem*. The word *Israeli* was found 58 times in these articles with the corpus frequency of 0.19%. The corpus frequency percentage, as calculated by the MonoConc Pro 2.2 software, computes the number of times a certain word was mentioned in the data set, divided by the total number of words in the corpus (all articles combined in that particular data set). So for this data set, there were a total of 31, 012 words analyzed, and *Israeli* was mentioned 58 times. The corpus frequency percentage was calculated by dividing 31, 012 by 58 and then multiplying by 100 to reach 0.19% (See Table 1). *Palestinian* was used 43 times with the rate of recurrence at 0.14%. The word *Israel* was utilized 42 times, at a rate of 0.14%. *Jerusalem* was found 41 times with the corpus frequency of 0.13%.

Table 1: Corpus Frequency List – Pre-9/11 Islam

Word	Count	Percentage
Israeli	58	0.19%
Palestinian	43	0.14%
Israel	42	0.14%
Jerusalem	41	0.13%

*Total count is the number of times the word appeared in the corpus. Total percentage is the percent of times this word appeared in the corpus.

The text surrounding the word *Islam* had corresponding patterns reflecting the religious conflict surrounding Jerusalem. In the articles, the most frequently-used word second-to- the-left of *Islam* was *Hamas*, (a Palestinian Islamist organization which loosely translates to "Islamic Resistance Movement") with the most frequently-used word that came directly before *Islam* being *Palestinian* (See Appendix B). The word *holy* was the most recurrent in coming directly after *Islam*[ic] (four times), followed by *republic* and *state* (three times), and *jihad* (two times). *War* was the most repetitively-used term second-to-the-right of the word *Islam* (four times), followed by *central* (three times), and *groups* (two times) (See Appendix B).

Pre-9/11 Muslim Data

Forty-seven articles were analyzed for the pre-9/11 *Muslim* category, out of which the word *Muslim* was cited 78 times. The most frequently-mentioned words (aside from the keyword *Muslim*) in this data set were *Israeli*, *Israel*, *government*, and *Palestinian*. The word *Israeli* was used the most frequently with 70 references, and a 0.20% rate of occurrence. *Israel* came in second with 55 mentions and a rate of 0.15%. *Government* was the third most-utilized word in the articles with 50 mentions and a corpus frequency of rate 0.14%, followed by *Palestinian* with 48 mentions and a rate of 0.13%.

Table 2: Corpus Frequency List – Pre-9/11 Muslim

Word	Count	Percentage
Israeli	70	0.20%
Israel	55	0.15%
Government	50	0.14%
Palestinian	48	0.13%

*Total count is the number of times the word appeared in the corpus. Total percentage is the percent of times this word appeared in the corpus.

The text surrounding the word *Muslim* did not have as much correlation with the frequency statistics in regards to the conflict in Jerusalem between Palestinians and Israelis. The most commonly-used words second-to-the-left of *Muslim* was *Arab*, with four mentions, followed by *Jews*, and *Christians* with three mentions each (See Appendix C). The word *convert* came directly before *Muslim* most frequently with four references, followed by *Afghan* and

Bosnian with three mentions each (See Appendix C). The word *group* was used most often immediately after the word *Muslim* with four references, along with *students* which had three mentions, followed by *mystics* and *political* with two references each (See Appendix C). *Christianity* was the most used word second-to-the-right of the word *Muslim* (four times), followed by *association* (two times) (See Appendix C).

Post-9/11 Islam Data

Post-9/11 data set uncovered 139 articles that contained the word *Islam*. This was almost three and a half times as many articles that were found for the pre-9/11 data set. In those articles, the word *Islam* was referenced 285 times. The most frequently-used words in these articles are as follows: *Against* was used 296 times (at a frequency rate of 0.26%), followed by *attacks* which was employed 293 times (0.26%), *Afghanistan* was used 287 times (0.25%), *Taliban* was referenced 261 times (0.23%), and *military* was utilized 250 times (0.22%).

Table 3: Corpus Frequency List – Post-9/11 Islam

Word	Count	Percentage
Against	296	0.26%
Attacks	293	0.26%
Afghanistan	287	0.25%
Taliban	261	0.23%
Military	250	0.22%

*Total count is the number of times the word appeared in the corpus. Total percentage is the percent of times this word appeared in the corpus.

The second-to-the-left word that was employed the most frequently before *Islam* was *war* with five references (See Appendix D). *Hamas* was used in the articles four times, followed by *attacks* and *Afghanistan* with three references each (See Appendix D). The words that came directly before *Islam* repeatedly were *militant*, with 17 references, *radical* and *against*, with eight references each, and *hard-line*, with five references (See Appendix D). *Jihad* and *groups* were the most often-used words that came immediately after *Islam* with 11 mentions each, followed by *world*, with eight references, and *group*, *militants*, and *extremists* each with seven mentions

27

(See Appendix D). *Groups* was the most used word <u>second-to-the-right</u> of *Islam* with nine references.

Post-9/11 Muslim Data

Employing systematic random sampling of selecting every fourth day, the word *Muslim* was found in 160 articles following the 9/11 attacks. Once again, this was almost three and a half times as many articles that were found for the pre-9/11 data set. There were 313 references to *Muslim* in the articles. The word *attacks* was used most frequently in these articles with 349 mentions, at a corpus frequency rate of 0.24%. The word *against* was employed the second most frequently with 345 references and a corpus frequency rate of 0.24%. The word *war* was used 310 times with a 0.22% rate of occurrence, followed by *Afghanistan*, which was utilized 304 times, at a rate of 0.21%. The word *Taliban* was mentioned 275 times, with a corpus frequency rate of 0.19%.

Table 4: Corpus Frequency List – Post-9/11 Muslim

Word	Count	Percentage
Attacks	349	0.24%
Against	345	0.24%
War	310	0.22%
Afghanistan	304	0.21%
Taliban	275	0.19%

*Total count is the number of times the word appeared in the corpus. Total percentage is the percent of times this word appeared in the corpus.

The word *Arab* was the most frequently-used term <u>second-to-the-left</u> of *Muslim* with five references, along with the words *for*, *against*, and *Arab-Americans* with four references each (See Appendix E). The word *American* came <u>directly before</u> *Muslim* most often with ten mentions, followed by *for* with nine mentions, *against* with six mentions, and *militant* with five mentions (See Appendix E). *Clerics* was the most-employed word <u>directly after</u> *Muslim* with 11 references, along with *world* coming in second with ten references, followed by *country* with eight mentions, *groups* with seven, and finally *Americans* with six mentions (See Appendix E).

28

The word that was used most frequently <u>second-to-the-right</u> of *Muslim* was *Arab* with four references (See Appendix E).

Summary of Results

Analyzing the pre-9/11 corpus frequency data uncovered that both *Islam* and *Muslim* articles had consistent usage of the words *Israeli*, *Palestinian*, and *Israel* (See Tables 1 & 2). Furthermore, when frequency statistics were evaluated side by side, the two sets of pre-9/11 data showed that the majority of these articles provided coverage of the religious turmoil in the Middle East with key words being: *Arab, Jews, Christians, political, Palestinian, holy, jihad, Hamas,* and *war* (See Appendices B & C). An example of this is evident in an excerpt from a pre-9/11 *Islam* article, where the journalist states: "The reference seemed to reflect a keen awareness that the Palestinian Authority, led by Yasir Arafat, was losing ground among Palestinians in the street to religion-based militant groups like Hamas and Islamic Jihad, or Islamic Holy War" (Haberman, 2001, August 13, p. 3). Another example can be found when analyzing a pre-9/11 *Muslim* article where the same journalist writes: "Abraham, rendered as Ibrahim in Arabic, is revered by Muslims as well as Jews, one reason that rival theological and nationalist claims collide here as they do nowhere else in the West Bank" (Haberman, 2001, August 25, p. 5). Therefore, it can be determined that descriptive texts surrounding the words *Islam* and *Muslim* in pre-9/11 articles were framed around the religious conflict between Israelis and Palestinians.

Analysis on the post-9/11 corpus frequency data found that both *Islam* and *Muslim* articles had reiterative use of the words *against, attacks, Afghanistan,* and *Taliban* (See Tables 3 & 4). The word *against* was used in the context of examining why someone would be *against* the United States or a debate on how to fight *against* terrorism. An example can be found in a post-9/11 *Muslim* article, where the reporter states: "The war against terrorism could require even more intermingling of political, military and economic interests" (Kahn, 2001, p. 12). The majority of the articles discussed *attacks* in the context of stating which countries and governments were condemning the 9/11 attacks. For example, in an article from the post-9/11 *Islam* data set titled "Condemnations from Arab Governments, but Widely Different Attitudes on the Street," the journalist states: "The official Saudi press agency said that such attacks "defy all religious values"" (MacFarquhar, 2001, p. 22).

29

Analysis of the frequency statistics revealed a few similarities between the post-9/11 *Islam* and *Muslim* articles. Both sets of articles included the recurring use of the words *militant* and *against* (See Appendices D and E). However, the word *Islam* was extensively embedded in violent frames through the frequent use of words like *radical, hard-line, extremists, jihad, war,* and *Hamas* (See Appendix D). For example, in an article from the post-9/11 *Islam* data set, journalist Burns writes: "Pakistan, a poor country of 140 million people awash in debt and Kalashnikovs--and now nuclear armed--has a growing number of destitute Muslims who have embraced the radical Islam of the Taliban as their only source of hope" (Burns, 2001, p. 5). Another example is evident in a post-9/11 *Islam* article where the journalist states: "Until recently, the Taliban have been useful to Pakistan, providing an ally on its western flank as rival India lurks to the east, and a breeding ground for Islamic militancy that could be redirected toward Kashmir" (Bearak, 2001, p. 1).

The usage of *Muslim* was overtly different with surrounding words including *Arab-Americans, American, women,* and *clerics* (See Appendix E). Interestingly enough, the word *American* was frequently used both before and after the word *Muslim* to identify opinions of *American Muslims* or *Muslim Americans* (See Appendix E). In an article titled, "Ties between a Mosque and Fort Bragg Stay Strong and Neighborly," the journalist discusses "… the Chicago-based Muslim Journal, whose Oct. 12 issue bears the large headline, "G-d Bless America, We are Muslim Americans Serving G-d and Country"" (Niebuhr, 2001, p. 8). An article analyzed for the post-9/11 *Muslim* data set describes the following: "The crowd rose to its feet when Imam Pasha pleaded for tolerance. "We are Muslims, but we are Americans," he declared. "We Muslims, Americans, stand today with a heavy weight on our shoulder that those who would dare do such dastardly acts claim our faith"" (McFadden, 2001, p. 7). Another example is evident in the article "Islam and Its Adherents Ride the Publicity Wave" when the reporter discusses a program called "Islam 101" aired on the *Oprah Winfrey Show*: ""Modern Muslim women!" Oprah Winfrey cheered at the end of her show yesterday, with the sense of triumph that her audience now saw that the phrase was not a contradiction" (James, 2001, p. 8). It can be established that post-9/11 articles portrayed *Islam* through a violent framework whereas *Muslim* was framed in the context of patriotism and understanding.

30

Chapter 5 – Discussion

The importance of investigating media content is that it becomes the starting point for identifying media influences and forecasting their effects. The results of this study show that pre-9/11 articles for both *Islam* and *Muslim* were framed around the conflict in Jerusalem between Muslims and Jews, which changed drastically in the post-9/11 data sets. It is also evident in the results that that reporters covered Islam-related stories using a violent frame whereas Muslim-related stories provided insight to the dual identities of Muslim Americans and their religious backgrounds, while promoting tolerance towards Muslims.

Post-hoc analysis was conducted on all four data sets in order to better deduce to what extent the aforementioned frames were employed for each keyword before and after the 9/11 attacks. The analysis was conducted by pulling out each sentence that included the keyword and counting how many of those sentences actually were related to the dominant frame prescribed, and then dividing that number by the total number of sentences found. For example, of the 139 post-9/11 *Islam* articles analyzed, there were 285 sentences found employing the keyword (*Islam*). Out of those 285 sentences, 175 sentences (61.40%) used *Islam* in the context of *extremists*, *war*, *militants*, *radical*, and *jihad*. Reporters James Risen and David Johnston write: "Today's attacks in New York and Washington bore the characteristics of past attacks linked to Mr. Bin Laden's group or their suspected allies in radical Islamic terrorism" (2001, p. 21). Coming in at a distant second, 20 sentences (7.01%) were found in the context of providing educational information about Islam, as noted by journalist Jim Rutenberg regarding the Music Television Channel (MTV): "It is also reporting on benefit concerts and producing short, educational segments on South Asian geography, Islam and military terms" (2001, p. 1). Twelve sentences (4.21%) mentioned anti-discriminatory messages and promoted peace and tolerance in the context of *Islam*. An example of this is evident in reporter Susan Sachs' article that states: "Despite calls for tolerance by President Bush after the terror attacks on Sept. 11, the groups' leaders said, people of Middle Eastern appearance in the United States have become targets of violence, bullying and discrimination" (2001, p. 27).

Of the 160 articles analyzed post-hoc for the post-9/11 *Muslim* category, 313 sentences were found with the keyword (*Muslim*). Out of the 313 sentences, 54 sentences (17.25%) contained peaceful messages either from Muslim American communities or about Muslim

American communities. For example, journalist Goodstein writes: "In the face of suspicion and discrimination, Muslims struggled to assert their identities as loyal American citizens and to say that their religion does not approve of violence against innocents" (2001, p. 12). Another 41 sentences (13.10%) were found that promoted the fair treatment of Muslim Americans and advocated anti-discriminatory practices against them. In the article "Fighting an Elusive Enemy," reporter David Kennedy writes: "The battle now joined will be waged on our soil, with all the attendant risk of collateral damage to the delicate fabric of democracy, as rising threats against Arab-Americans and Muslims, and cries for restrictions on civil liberties, already portend" (2001, p. 11). From this set of articles, 21 sentences (6.71%) carried messages of Muslims living harmoniously with people of other faiths.

The importance of investigating frames employed in news content is constructive so that media effects of such frames can be measured. The newspaper study conducted by Vergeers, Lubbers, and Scheepers (2000) demonstrated how different newspapers can cultivate peoples' perceptions of ethnic minorities Similarly, it is possible that the frames found in this *New York Times'* research produced adverse attitudes towards Islam, and appeasing opinions towards Muslims. This research can be linked to a segment of the second prong of Gerbner and Gross' (1976) Cultural Indicators research where *message system analysis* is utilized to quantify and measure recurring representations of violence and minorities in media content. The repeated employment of violent frames found in the post-9/11 *Islam* data set indicate that media content proactively implements bias to unsuspecting recipients.

The findings of this research also coincide with Reynolds and Barnett's (2003) qualitative study of CNN's new coverage in the 12 hours following the 9/11 attacks. Two of the three main thematic clusters uncovered in Reynolds and Barnett's (2003) study comprised of elements of violence and strong war rhetoric. One thematic cluster involved strong references to war and military response, whereas the other cluster incorporated justification themes for rapid retaliation (Reynolds & Barnett, 2003). In the days following the 9/11 attacks, U.S. President Bush cautioned Americans that "this crusade, this war on terrorism, is going to take awhile" (Ford, 2001). The President's reference to a *crusade* ignited apprehension throughout American and the rest of the world, prompting the French foreign minister, Hubert Vedrine, to respond with the following statement: "We have to avoid a clash of civilizations at all costs" (Ford, 2001). Again,

32

this type of war rhetoric corresponds with the results of the post-9/11 *Islam* data set, where violent frames were employed in the context of Islam.

The post-9/11 *Muslim* data concurs with the research conducted by Nacos and Torres-Reyna (2003), in which four newspapers were analyzed to measure if media used negative and stereotypical frames in covering Muslim Americans. Nacos and Torres-Reyna (2003) found that, overall, Muslim Americans were depicted in a more favorable manner after the 9/11 attacks and the majority of the articles consisted issues of civil liberties and civil rights. The post-9/11 *Muslim* data set also exhibited more positive coverage of Muslims, with the dominant frame emphasizing conciliation and unity as Americans.

The Council on American-Islamic Relations (CAIR), a Washington-based national civil rights and advocacy organization, conducted a survey almost three years after the 9/11 attacks to measure how Americans perceive Muslims (CAIR, 2004). The poll was conducted through telephone interviews in June and July of 2004 and included a random-sampling of 1,000 American households (CAIR, 2004). Results indicated that one out of every four American polled believed in negative stereotypes such as "Muslims teach their children to hate" and "Muslims value life less than other people" (CAIR, 2004). The CAIR study also found that negative images of Muslims were 16 times more prevalent than positive ones. The CAIR study results, measured almost three years after the 9/11 attacks, were in stark contrast to the analysis of the post-9/11 *Muslim* data set which consisted of New York Times articles published in the one month following the attacks. This suggests a shift in Americans' perception of Muslims from the weeks following the 9/11 attacks to three years later.

In a 2004 national study conducted by the Media and Society Research Group and Cornell University, participants were surveyed about their knowledge of Islam (Media and Society Research Group, 2004). Researchers asked respondents to either agree or disagree with the following two statements:

1. Islamic values and beliefs are very similar to Western/Christian values and beliefs.

2. The Islamic religion is more likely than others to encourage violence among its believers. Results showed that 27% of the participants agreed with the first statement regarding similarities in values and beliefs between Muslims and Christians, while 73% disagreed. Forty-seven percent of the participants agreed with the second statement that Islam promoted more violence than other religions (Media and Society Research Group, 2004).

The researchers also gauged participants' basic knowledge of Islam by asking the following two questions:

1. What is the name Muslims use to refer to God? (Allah)
2. What is the Islamic equivalent to the Bible? (Qur'an)

Out of the 100 respondents surveyed, 54 answered both questions correctly, 20 answered one question correctly, and 26 people answered neither question correctly (Media and Society Research Group, 2004). The results of the Media and Society Research Group study helps make transparent the need for accurate reporting, as there is sufficient proof in the data compiled here that Islam is framed as a violent religion.

It is important to note that though Islam is the second-largest religion in the world today, a good portion of Americans are ignorant about basic knowledge of this religion and its followers (Media and Society Research Group, 2004). The content analysis conducted on the post-9/11 *Islam* articles also substantiates the claim that this religion is stereotyped as violent, given that 61.40% of the sentences written (with *Islam* in them) were in the context of *extremists, war, militants, radical,* and *jihad.* However, it must be acknowledged that the post-9/11 *Muslim* articles did not propagate a violent frame, and, instead, 17.25% of the sentences (with the word *Muslim* in them) established non-violent, conciliatory messages regarding Muslim Americans. Perhaps the reason that Islam was framed in a violent manner, whereas the people of its' faith were attributed with more placatory traits, had to do with the fact that the religion of Islam was foreign to most Americans up until that point, whereas Muslim Americans shared at least one major commonality, their country.

Limitations/Suggestions for Future Research

A major limitation in this research involved the large quantities of articles found for the post-9/11 data set. Initially this study had included the following keywords for analysis: *Pakistani, Taliban, extremist, Saudi, Palestinian, Arab, Middle Eastern,* and *terrorist* in order to explore a more comprehensive range of terms. However, preliminary investigation using the online search engine LexisNexis Academic found such a huge quantity of articles that it would have been impossible to manage for the purpose and scope of this research. The total number of articles for the pre-9/11 data set would have totaled 497 and the post-9/11 data set to a whopping 2,745+. Even with the use of systematic random sampling, the database of articles to analyze would have been entirely too much and so all the terms were eliminated from analysis, with the exception of *Islam* and *Muslim*. Future studies will benefit from analyzing specific ethnicities and violent terms (such as *terrorist* and *extremist*), along with the context in which particular ethnic groups and violent terms are employed. Also, even with the two words used for this study (*Islam* and *Muslim*), 253 articles were found for the pre-9/11 data set and 1,318 articles were found for the post-9/11 data set. It became necessary to use systematic random sampling in order to reduce the number of articles making the analysis more manageable. Once again, future studies will be more descriptive if all 1,517 articles are included in the assessment.

Another limitation of this study was the inability to incorporate the framing techniques using Ashley and Olson's (1998) categories of *importance, illegitimacy, deviance,* and *event coverage.* Again, this was hindered due to the number of articles being analyzed. In order to fully inspect every article against the Ashley and Olson (1998) categories, more time and additional resources would have been required to gauge the data effectively. However, it would have been beneficial to this study to delve into the *importance* category in which the amount of coverage each word receives, story topics, and section placements of the articles are analyzed (Ashley & Olson, 1998; Shoemaker, 1984). This would have been especially constructive given the amount of articles found not just for the *Islam* and *Muslim* articles, but also the omitted terms listed above. The category of *deviance* would have also enhanced this research as it deals with analysis of the subjects (in this case, Muslims and Islam) being shown as deviants, with an emphasis on violence (Ashley & Olson, 1998; Gitlin, 2003). Last, *event coverage* could have helped determine to what extent events of Islamic nature and Muslims were the focus of the articles rather than the issues of the two social groups (Ashley & Olson, 1998; Staggenborg, 1993).

Another limitation of this research was that factual news articles and opinion pieces (such as editorials and letters-to-the-editor) were collapsed for analysis. Future studies could benefit from conducting separate assessments of fact-based articles and opinion-based articles. Qualitative content analysis of framing techniques requires subjective research and being a Muslim American myself, it is possible that personal biases and interpretations affected this study.

Also, this research only examined one elite American publication, the *New York Times*, whereas analysis of an international newspaper may produced have varied results. In future studies, multiple newspaper sources could be investigated to distinguish similarities and variances between national, international, and local news coverage. Television has become the most popular source of providing information and future studies would benefit from examining framing distinctions between newspaper and television coverage (Stempel & Hargrove, 2002; Berger, 1995). Finally, it is a limitation that the news media tends to focus on negative items much more than positive ones which could have impacted the results of this study (Media Research Center, 2005). With a large-scale brutal tragedy such as the 9/11/2001 attacks, it can be argued that the violent frames employed by the *New York Times* were newsworthy.

Conclusion

There is substantial evidence that through the process of framing, media communicates persuasively to its viewers (Bracci, 2003; Maslog, Lee, & Kim, 2006; Tankard et al., 1991). Alongside a technological and information proliferation where the Internet, satellite news, citizen journalism, and even cell phone cameras encompass what is considered news, journalists must adhere to vigilant standards. Also, most estimates for the Muslim American population vary from three to six million people, with experts agreeing that these figures will continue to rise (Haque, 2004). Considering the post-9/11 significance of global media, along with the growing Muslim American population in the United States, this research aimed to measure the frames used by *New York Times'* journalists when covering stories related to *Islam* and *Muslim.* Research revealed that pre-9/11 *Islam* and *Muslim* articles were framed around the religious conflict in Jerusalem, between Israelis and Palestinians. The context of post-9/11 *Islam* articles were embedded in violent references, while post-9/11 *Muslim* articles were framed around patriotism and tolerance. Further research is necessary to thoroughly inspect the correlation between the media's depiction of Islam and its' followers and the social ramifications it carries. The bias towards Islam and Muslims in American media has a tumultuous history. However, it is necessary to maintain neutral positions when reporting about ethnic groups and religions in order to prevent frameworks from developing into facts and beliefs.

Appendix A: 30-Day Timeline Post-9/11*

09/12/01   Hijackers crash two airliners into the World Trade Center in New York. A third strikes the Pentagon, and a fourth crashes in a field in rural Pennsylvania. More than 3,000 people are killed in the terror attacks.

09/13/01   The White House announces that there is "overwhelming evidence" that Osama bin Laden is behind the attacks.

09/14/01   Congress authorizes President George W. Bush to use "all necessary and appropriate force against those nations, organizations, or persons he determines planned, authorized, committed, or aided the terrorist attacks that occurred on September 11, 2001, or harbored such organizations or persons, in order to prevent any future acts of international terrorism against the United States by such nations, organizations or persons."

09/16/01   Osama bin Laden denies any involvement in the 9/11 attacks in a statement to Al-Jazeera television, saying, "I would like to assure the world that I did not plan the recent attacks, which seems to have been planned by people for personal reasons."

09/18/01   The Justice Department publishes an interim regulation allowing non-citizens suspected of terrorism to be detained without charge for 48 hours or "an additional reasonable period of time" in the event of an "emergency or other extraordinary circumstance." The new rule is used to hold hundreds indefinitely until the USA Patriot Act passes in October.

09/20/01   President Bush announces the new cabinet-level Office of Homeland Security, to be led by Pennsylvania Governor Tom Ridge. Ridge later becomes secretary of a new Homeland Security Department.

In an address to a joint session of Congress, President Bush declares, "Every nation, in every region, now has a decision to make. Either you are with us, or you are with the terrorists. From this day forward, any nation that continues to harbor or support terrorism will be regarded by the United States as a hostile regime."

10/02/01   The USA Patriot Act is introduced in Congress.

10/04/01   British Prime Minister Tony Blair, speaking before an emergency session of Parliament, says that three of the nineteen 9/11 hijackers have been positively identified as "known associates" of Osama bin Laden.

10/05/01   One thousand soldiers from the U.S. Army's 10th Mountain Division are sent to the Central Asian nation of Uzbekistan, which borders Afghanistan.

10/05/01	A photographer for the tabloid newspaper *The Sun* dies of inhalation anthrax in Boca Raton, Florida. Over the next several weeks, along with several false alarms, four other letters containing anthrax are received, by NBC News, the New York Post, Senate Majority Leader Tom Daschle (D-SD) and Senator Patrick Leahy (D-VT). Eleven people are infected; five people die.
10/07/01	The U.S. begins bombing Afghanistan. In a televised address, President Bush tells the nation: "On my orders, the United States military has begun strikes against al Qaeda terrorist training camps and military installations of the Taliban regime in Afghanistan. These carefully targeted actions are designed to disrupt the use of Afghanistan as a terrorist base of operations, and to attack the military capability of the Taliban regime."

*Timeline duplicated from the following website:
Public Broadcasting Station. (n. d.) *In focus: This moment in history: Post 9/11 timeline.* Retrieved 02/11/2007 from:
http://www.pbs.org/flashpointsusa/20040629/infocus/topic_01/timeline_sep2001.html

Appendix B: Frequency Statistics Pre-9/11 – Islam

	2-Left		1-Left		1-Right		2-Right
4	**of**	**8**	**the**	**5**	**in**	**4**	**war**
2	in	7	and	4	holy	4	the
2	hamas	7	an	3	state	4	and
2	to	6	of	3	republic	3	in
2	the	3	palestinian	2	rule	3	central
2	a	2	in	2	jihad	2	to
1	behind	2	for	2	court	2	groups
1	interpretation	1	two	2	and	1	that
1	against	1	include	2	that	1	–
1	rocked	1	b	1	regime	1	aiding
1	blamed	1	editor	1	activists	1	fighting
1	villagers	1	traditional	1	from	1	have
1	pakistan	1	renouncing	1	law	1	blamed
1	outlawed	1	face	1	religion	1	successful
1	exploit	1	sure	1	militants	1	five
1	world's	1	only	1	if	1	various
1	anti-arabism	1	purist	1	groups	1	system
1	anti-semitism	1	strict	1	worldwide	1	hats
1	mistake	1	to	1	legal	1	traces
1	mourning	1	militant	1	styles	1	here
1	european	1	that	1	fundamentalist	1	a
1	praised	1	different	1	live	1	copyright
1	not	1	fantasies	1	as	1	of
1	taliban's	1	or	1	much	1	mr
1	offshoot	1	practice	1	judges	1	local
1	workers	1	pakistani-backed	1	seem	1	needs
1	iran	1	headline	1	morals	1	those
1	jerusalem	1	on	1	have	1	it
1	like	1	by	1	group	1	police
1	me			1	contains	1	like
1	survive			1	palestinian	1	been
1	sympathetic			1	has	1	leaders
1	into			1	militant	1	once
1	god			1	one	1	hamas
1	headline			1	guerrilla	1	are
1	reverence			1	areas	1	sheik
1	within			1	unfortunately	1	forgotten

31,012 words, 6,809 types

39

Appendix C: Frequency Statistics Pre-9/11 – Muslim

MonoConc Pro - [Frequency Statistics - [*Muslim*]]

File Concordance Frequency Display Window Info

2-Left		1-Left		1-Right		2-Right	
6	the	10	and	6	in	6	the
6	to	8	the	4	to	4	christianity
5	of	6	of	4	group	3	in
4	a	5	a	3	students	3	that
4	arab	4	convert	3	and	3	and
3	jews	3	afghan	3	the	2	association
3	with	3	bosnian	2	political	2	have
3	christians	2	000	2	population	2	roofs
2	7	2	my	2	mystics	2	to
2	christianity	2	or	2	it	1	at
1	counteract	2	whether	2	who	1	violation
1	against	2	to	1	general	1	know
1	this	2	not	1	dynasty	1	timetable
1	camps	1	hard-line	1	pro-palestinian	1	made
1	who	1	national	1	as	1	intolerant
1	changes	1	by	1	men	1	summed
1	if	1	these	1	no	1	pro-jerusalem
1	revered	1	this	1	nation	1	well
1	as	1	their	1	kids	1	benjamin
1	ulema	1	black	1	scholars	1	not
1	massacre	1	mainly	1	or	1	said
1	are	1	jewish	1	he	1	turbaned
1	or	1	for	1	delegates	1	copyright
1	violence	1	against	1	officials	1	was
1	rooms	1	small	1	worship	1	had
1	faith	1	killing	1	eighteen	1	arab
1	chanting	1	over	1	rebellion	1	people
1	become	1	american	1	fundamentalist	1	left
1	coalition	1	with	1	party	1	protects
1	recall	1	be	1	worshipers	1	kashmir
1	for	1	some	1	minister	1	terror
1	business	1	night	1	changed	1	but
1	morass	1	arab	1	support	1	his
1	many	1	shiite	1	chaplain	1	i
1	test	1	peace-loving	1	voters	1	after
1	join	1	are	1	matter	1	who
1	sufis	1	sunni	1	groups	1	share

221.05 kbytes, 1 file

Appendix D: Frequency Statistics Post-9/11 – Islam

MonoConc Pro - [Frequency Statistics - [*Islam*]]

File   Concordance   Frequency   Display   Window   Info

2-Left		1-Left		1-Right		2-Right	
20	the	36	the	17	and	23	the
19	of	31	of	11	groups	17	in
10	to	18	and	11	jihad	16	and
8	by	17	militant	8	world	13	of
7	a	13	on	7	is	9	a
5	in	8	by	7	group	9	that
5	war	8	against	7	extremists	9	have
4	and	8	radical	7	militants	9	groups
4	hamas	7	to	6	movement	6	to
3	attacks	7	an	5	the	5	has
3	afghanistan	5	hard-line	5	fundamentalist	5	who
3	from	5	about	4	itself	5	for
3	west	4	that	4	clerics	5	but
3	accusations	4	for	4	radicals	5	are
3	or	3	as	4	taliban	4	there
3	with	3	with	4	in	4	it
2	jamiat	3	in	4	terrorism	4	is
2	attack	3	not	4	a	3	as
2	taliban	2	among	4	militant	3	with
2	years	2	or	4	leaders	2	all
2	it	2	ulema	4	terror	2	they
2	is	2	from	3	militancy	2	muslims
2	afghanistan's	2	between	3	schools	2	many
2	threat	2	pakistan-based	3	center	2	at
2	states	2	armed	3	101	2	from
2	as	2	egyptian	3	countries	2	mr
2	not	2	egypt's	3	terrorists	2	government
2	for	1	clear	3	state	2	was
2	billed	1	nonviolent	3	rule	2	arab
2	expert	1	link	2	culture	2	its
2	curiosity	1	two	2	was	2	front
1	controlled	1	worldwide	2	of	2	sites
1	koran	1	american	2	law	2	movement
1	adherents	1	their	2	terrorist	2	hamas
1	name	1	pure	2	threat	2	he
1	early	1	moderate	2	conference	2	–
1	up	1	which	2	guerrilla	2	say

690.83 kbytes, 1 file

41

Appendix E: Frequency Statistics Post-9/11 – Muslim

MonoConc Pro - [Frequency Statistics - [*Muslim*]]							

File Concordance Frequency Display Window Info

2-Left		1-Left		1-Right		2-Right	
18	of	29	the	29	and	15	the
13	the	23	a	11	clerics	13	in
10	a	19	and	10	in	12	who
8	and	17	of	10	world	11	and
8	by	10	american	9	who	10	that
7	in	9	for	8	country	9	to
6	to	7	by	7	groups	6	he
6	with	6	that	6	americans	6	we
5	arab	6	to	5	women	5	of
4	for	6	against	5	populations	4	a
4	against	5	militant	5	the	4	not
4	as	4	predominantly	4	nations	4	from
4	arab-americans	3	are	4	travelers	4	arab
3	islam	3	radical	4	countries	3	are
3	mostly	3	mainstream	4	nation	3	whose
3	said	3	mostly	3	state	3	on
3	among	3	many	3	brotherhood	3	is
3	that	2	million	3	to	3	sikhs
3	one	2	some	3	is	3	said
2	center	2	–	3	from	3	–
2	across	2	largest	3	cleric	3	has
2	from	2	on	3	group	3	have
2	most	2	other	2	leaders	3	but
2	jewish	2	at	2	today	3	christians
2	are	2	fellow	2	he	3	like
2	not	2	any	2	but	3	jews
2	nation	2	traditional	2	political	3	mr
2	past	2	said	2	terrorists	3	body
2	is	2	local	2	girl	2	terrorism
2	lawyer	2	defending	2	guerrillas	2	since
2	linked	2	from	2	extremists	2	by
2	140	2	if	2	that	2	had
2	any	2	populous	2	or	2	groups
2	we	2	shiite	2	woman	2	month
2	other	2	both	2	as	2	native
2	backlash	2	sunni	2	would	2	people
2	on			2	christians	2	makes

863.90 kbytes, 1 file

Appendix F: Concordance Sample Screen Shot Pre-9/11 – Islam

```
MonoConc Pro - [Concordance - [*Islam*]]                                    [_][□][X]
File  Concordance  Frequency  Display  Sort  Window  Info                      [_][□][x]
```

st suicide bombing, offered for the glory of God and Islam. From the Palestinian village across the road comes
I resist that linkage, because I've known a different Islam. In the year before the current intifada began, I unde
or Muslim mystics, on the periphery of Palestinian Islam. One sheik dismissed rival Israeli and Palestinian te
hoing a rabbinic teaching. In showing reverence for Islam, I was able to elicit a reciprocal gesture from some M
as a reservist soldier in Nuseirat, the heartland of Islamic extremism, and had been hit in the head with a rock
ry – and sadly marginal – voices within Palestinian Islam have been intimidated into silence. Clergy on Palest
r faith is sullied. Today, my forays into Palestinian Islam seem like fantasies. Islam has once again become u
y forays into Palestinian Islam seem like fantasies. Islam has once again become untouchable, pervasive and
o Israeli leader denies the sanctity of Jerusalem for Islam, Palestinian leaders have repudiated the historical c
h people. Still, my religious journey taught me that Islam contains those qualities necessary for peacemaking
ingers some Jews who believe it is sympathetic to Islamic militant groups. In response, Mrs. Clinton returned :
erical conservatives recognize that to survive, the Islamic Republic needs to produce better economic results.
al supporters, have keenly felt the pressure of the Islamic morals police intruding on their daily lives. Conserv
ians is probably the greatest threat to the future of Islamic rule. It is in the clerics' interest to ease the suffocat
i intelligence officer who specializes in the militant Islamic group Hamas, knew instantly that a bomb had been
. The only death was that of the bomber, whom the Islamic Holy War group claimed as one of its own. Even wi
Jerusalem, one of the most important holy sites in Islam. The reference seemed to reflect a keen awareness t
et to religion-based militant groups like Hamas and Islamic Jihad, or Islamic Holy War. So concerned is Mr. Ara
d militant groups like Hamas and Islamic Jihad, or Islamic Holy War. So concerned is Mr. Arafat about his star
about his standing that he has invited Hamas and Islamic Jihad to join him in a coalition – a unity governmen'
ie assets" if he does not do more to crack down on Islamic terrorists and their sponsors. Four Hamas member:
losives strapped to his chest. He was identified by Islamic Holy War as Muhammad Mahmoud Nasr, 28, from (
tianity." The Taliban, who espouse a strict brand of Islam that considers attempts to convert Muslims a crime,
letails, that they had arrested three members of an Islamic Holy War"terrorist cell" who were planning "a large-
itorial Desk; Pg. 22 LENGTH: 440 words HEADLINE: Islam in Central Asia BODY: The people of Uzbekistan, Tu
n is leading a regionwide crackdown on all forms of Islam that are not state-controlled – repression that is drivi
ito opposition and forcing religion underground. An Islamic guerrilla movement seeks to establish an Islamic s
i Islamic guerrilla movement seeks to establish an Islamic state in Uzbekistan, but its 1,000 or so fighters are
millions of people in Central Asia began to practice Islam. Unfortunately, local governments saw religion that v
accused of violent acts. Thousands of villagers in Islamic areas have been forcibly resettled. The current gue
ired terrorism." India has blamed Pakistani-backed Islamic militants fighting Indian rule in the Indian state of Ja
y obstacle to better relations between Pakistan, an Islamic state, and India. Pakistan maintains that the 12-yea
harges of "forming a group that aims to exploit the Islamic religion to propagate extremist ideas." All have plea
': A day after Pakistan's military ruler outlawed two Islamic groups blamed for sectarian killings, the police arre
TORIAL A22-23 Editorials: The chancellor gets a B+; Islam in Central Asia; Verlyn Klinkenborg on mosquitoes. C
al proceedings over the murders, which rocked the Islamic republic. Five of the agents, including middle-level
IEADLINE: Uzbek Crackdown BODY: To the Editor: "Islam in Central Asia" (editorial, Aug. 16) suggests that the
e Uzbekistan government's stand behind traditional Islam, if successful, should only contribute to peace in the
men's refusal to widen the investigation to include Islamic activists. The Times had said the refusal essentiall

| 57 matches | Original text order | Strings matching: *Islam* |

G:\Media\Other Shared Documents\Research\pre911Islam.txt   187.63 kbytes, 1 file

Appendix G: Concordance Sample Screen Shot Pre-9/11 – Muslim

MonoConc Pro - [Concordance - ["Muslim"]]

File   Concordance   Frequency   Display   Sort   Window   Info

kullcap as a religious Jew, I was invited to join the Muslim prayer line. My goal wasn't to blur the borders betw
blur the borders between faiths but to test whether Muslims and Jews could share a common language of devo
found eager partners – mostly among the Sufis, or Muslim mystics, on the periphery of Palestinian Islam. One
I was able to elicit a reciprocal gesture from some Muslims, who acknowledged that the return of the Jews to Is
rred during the festival of Lailat al-Miraj, the night Muslims believe that Muhammad ascended to heaven from
ed bombs, march in processions of martyrdom. My Muslim friends are unable to publicly express their shame
uchable, pervasive and elusive as air. Many Arab Muslims, encouraged by official media and leading clergy, r
less awareness of mortality. I know that Jews and Muslims can share wisdom, if not doctrine. Even as suicide
ronts a war that is being forced upon it, I recall the Muslim mystics who opened their doors and their hearts to
dorsement given by a large, organized coalition of Muslim voters in New York City and won the support of a sr
a news release rescinding the endorsement of the Muslim group after a Jewish assemblyman linked it to terro
d or did not have an endorsement meeting with the Muslim group that then put its support behind Mr. Green – tl
id he thought he was meeting with advocates for a Muslim chaplain for the Fire Department. Now this week, ea
not say to people they did or did not believe to be Muslim political activists. "The ethnic minefield of New Yorl
or Senate when she was drawn into a morass over Muslim support. During the campaign for Senate last year,
zed by the Massachusetts chapter of the American Muslim Alliance, a group that angers some Jews who believ
The inability for any candidate to do business with Muslim groups without taking heat raises questions about v
rithout taking heat raises questions about whether Muslims, who have gained some political power in places li
foreign policy," said Clifford Chanin, an expert on Muslims in Western cultures and president of a nonprofit re:
unty and a registered Republican. Also in July, the Muslim Political Coordinating Committee of New York said t
said Joe DePlasco, Mr. Green's spokesman. The Muslim matter did not end there. The following day, three of
BODY: Three former commanders of the Bosnian Muslim army pleaded not guilty before the United Nations v
aws of war. They are the highest-ranking Bosnian Muslims yet to appear before the tribunal. Copyright 2001 T
erusalem (around 1895-1900), sacred to Jews and Muslims; the roofs of the city of Aleppo, Syria, around 1900;
nspiracy by Western aid groups to convert Afghan Muslims. The Taliban foreign minister, Wakil Ahmed Muttaw
es and organizations to try to convert good Afghan Muslims to Christianity." The Taliban, who espouse a strict
brand of Islam that condemns attempts to convert Muslims a crime, arrested 8 foreign workers and 16 Afghan :
er Now to distribute as a means of enticing Afghan Muslims to Christianity. "The W.F.P. should be ready to ans
ization was doing and that it was trying to convert Muslims," Mr. Muttawakil said. A World Food Program spoki
e government has arrested thousands of religious Muslims and sentenced hundreds of them to long jail terms,
e of government actions. When the mass arrest of Muslims began in 1997, young religious men went undergro
small one in 1999. India considers predominantly Muslim Kashmir an integral part of the nation, while Pakista
unal to face charges of murder and persecution of Muslims while serving near the eastern Bosnian town of Sre
own of Srebrenica in 1995, where more than 7,000 Muslims were massacred. Lt. Col. Dragan Jokic turned hims
vez Musharraf banned Lashkar-e-Jhangvi, a Sunni Muslim group, and Sipah-e-Mohammed, a Shiite Muslim gro
ni Muslim group, and Sipah-e-Mohammed, a Shiite Muslim group, and threatened to ban other violent groups. C
d him how he feels about his relationship with the Muslims being summed up by his being "a useful idiot . . . ti
erican. When successful, it changes peace-loving Muslims into intolerant political activists. Wahhabism has ;
ho are Orthodox, nor the ethnic Albanians, who are Muslim, have made religion an overt part of the conflict heri

| 78 matches | Original text order | Strings matching: "Muslim" |

221.05 kbytes, 1 file

Appendix H: Concordance Sample Screen Shot Post-9/11 – Islam

MonoConc Pro - [Concordance - [*Islam*]]

File   Concordance   Frequency   Display   Sort   Window   Info

ntal rugs and stocked with copies of the Koran and Islamic literature. The room is mostly used by Muslim trave
of Mullah Fazlur Rehman, who heads Jamiat Ulema Islam, a hard-line Islamic political party that supports Afgh
hman, who heads Jamiat Ulema Islam, a hard-line Islamic political party that supports Afghanistan's Taliban r
not in a border city or a city strongly controlled by Islamic radicals, but just minutes away from , the capital, a
, the Saudi-born terrorism suspect, so tightly to the Islamic faith that an attack on him would be seen as an atta
hat an attack on him would be seen as an attack on Islam itself. Rawalpindi is also where the Pakistani Army i:
tates was not after Mr. bin Laden or the Taliban but Islam itself. Muslims in Pakistan, he said, should ignore M
hey believed that Mr. bin Laden was a champion of Islam, if not more. "Osama talks to Allah," said Midrarul Ha
iban government, but not ordinary Afghans or their Islamic faith." Mr. Blair, who has committed British forces to
are his victims, too. Still less is it directed against Islam. I want to make it clear. Islam is a peaceful religion.
is it directed against Islam. I want to make it clear. Islam is a peaceful religion. "The vast majority of Muslim:
ng the government ward off pressures from militant Islamic groups over General Musharraf's commitment to su
ng that he considers Mr. bin Laden – a hero among Islamic militants in Pakistan – to be a murderer, the phrasir
ote the curiosity that has suddenly sprung up about Islam, a faith with about a billion adherents worldwide. "Isl
n, a faith with about a billion adherents worldwide. "Islam is in the air," said Imam Shakir, speaking to about 3!
bin Laden, who has claimed to fight in the name of Islam. Indeed, many within the mosque, which serves a c
ntry." The mosque is named for an early American Islamic figure, Omar Ibn Sayyid, a West African sold into sl
rassing phone calls from people who wanted to link Islam itself with the terrorism. But there were no outright th
his long ties to the United States to keeping militant Islam in check. Conversations here often start with fond rei
ainst what he saw as America's "unfair" war against Islam. He is a Palestinian refugee from Hebron. He wrote c
alliance has won 202 districts, including 18 by two Islamic fundamentalist allies, from the 283 seats where und
ents understand the whole issue, that this is not an Islamic problem but a terrorist problem." Mr. Ahmed, an Am
s HEADLINE: A NATION CHALLENGED: THE MEDIA; Islam and Its Adherents Ride the Publicity Wave BYLINE: I
s, right?" she asked one her guests, a professor of Islamic studies. The program, billed as "Islam 101," was o
ofessor of Islamic studies. The program, billed as "Islam 101," was one of the latest responses to the country
Western dress, Ms. Winfrey set about demystifying Islam and going past the knee-jerk pleas against discrimin
onversation. The evidence of a new curiosity about Islam is all around. Last night PBS began repeating "Islam
lam is all around. Last night PBS began repeating "Islam: Empire of Faith," a historical series first shown in M
Amazon.com's best-seller list was "Taliban: Militant Islam, Oil and Fundamentalism in Central Asia," a book pu
osition as her viewers, she said, "We're calling this Islam 101 because we're figuring that a lot of you all, just I
, including the information that the religion is called Islam and its followers are called Muslims. She also noted
up with you." The show began by focusing on what Islam shares with other cultures, emphasizing that Muslim
ssed because of government decrees, not because Islam requires it. Ever attuned to her audience and using h
s for Mr. Sharon. Though any declaration of war on Islamic and Arab terrorism should delight Israelis – and did
nconditionally shared its extensive intelligence on Islamic terror groups with the United States, they said, Mr. :
ering from liver disease in Algeria, and he defended Islam over Christianity. Mr. Raissi was often seen in the c
Taliban, not the Afghan people and particularly not Islam. Secretary of Defense Donald H. Rumsfeld finished
e with Washington against its fears of uprisings by Islamic populations deeply suspicious of America's real go
orders southern Afghanistan, but its rulers, the first Islamic government to accept America's case that Mr. bin L

| 285 matches | Original text order | Strings matching: *Islam* |

690.83 kbytes, 1 file

Appendix I: Concordance Sample Screen Shot Post-9/11 – Muslim

MonoConc Pro - [Concordance - [*Muslim*]]

File   Concordance   Frequency   Display   Sort   Window   Info

ted that suicide attacks are not condoned by most Muslims, but are espoused "by leaders of religious factions
OF TERROR: THE TIES; In U.S., Echoes of Rift Of Muslims and Jews BYLINE: By LAURIE GOODSTEIN BODY
nd Jews BYLINE: By LAURIE GOODSTEIN BODY: Muslim women in headscarves were advised to stay indoor
arves were advised to stay indoors. Mosques and Muslim schools in Los Angeles were shut down, and Muslir
uslim schools in Los Angeles were shut down, and Muslim leaders in Michigan and other states reported recei
struck New York City and Washington yesterday, Muslims and Arab-Americans in the New York region and ac
onates particular repercussions here among both Muslims and Jews, whose kin in the Middle East are locked
ores. In the face of suspicion and discrimination, Muslims struggled to assert their identities as loyal America
homa." The news revived fresh memories among Muslims and Arab-Americans of the aftermath of the Oklahor
ity bombing in 1995, when snap judgment blamed Muslim terrorists, and mosques were defaced, Muslim trave
ed Muslim terrorists, and mosques were defaced, Muslim travelers detained in airports, and families harasse
se if it was, repercussions would follow. American Muslim and Arab organizations rushed to condemn the atta
first plane hit the World Trade Center. "American Muslims utterly condemn what are apparently vicious and c
errorism against innocent civilians," the American Muslim Political Coordination Council said in a statement. "
el "is too high a price to pay." For both Jewish and Muslim Americans, some of the most disturbing television i
mages from Palestinian towns and refugee camps, Muslim and Arab leaders in the New York area emphasized
s held as scheduled. Across the nation, prominent Muslims reported receiving phone calls from worried men an
be better to say that it is the Ottoman Empire, not Muslims per se, that haunts Narnia. Lewis mocks the old pic
prevent discrimination against Arab-Americans or Muslims? A. It's normal to be angry at what happened and to
ns had not been combat, but merely to celebrate a Muslim holiday. But it was not the explosives per se that w
ys, it was pitted dirt roads replete with land mines, Muslim clerics and AK-47's that seemed normal while life in
acy, as rising threats against Arab-Americans and Muslims, and cries for restrictions on civil liberties, already
battle against terrorism, like Indonesia, the largest Muslim nation. "The terrorists obviously understood the An
gious and social institutions as well as individual Muslims the targets of violence and vandalism. Though the
y and a longtime student of race and racism, "and Muslims have become even more of a designated 'other' tha
re of a designated 'other' than blacks. We look at Muslims as dangerous aliens who won't fit in and can't fit in
ssor at American University, said that "noncitizen Muslims" would be vulnerable because "under the immigrat
bhorred by religious fundamentalists (and not only Muslim fundamentalists) as licentiousness, corruption, gree
e imaginations of virtually everyone – one reason Muslim fundamentalists so hate America.They certainly und
: is expecting a backlash against Arab-Americans, Muslims and immigrants from the Middle East. The telephor
nya has shown, it also sees a threat to the mostly Muslim provinces like Tajikistan, poor and militarily weak re
REAL; A Sense of Foreboding in Canada's Diverse Muslim Haven BYLINE: By BARBARA CROSSETTE DATELI
attend. In neighborhoods all over Montreal where Muslim families have been living in harmony with families
eliminated. This city has one of Canada's largest Muslim populations, about 100,000 people. There is a sens
still prevails, Islamic leaders say, a drumbeat of anti-Muslim invective has been coming from some radio talk s
their midst. If you are insulted because you are a Muslim, he advised them, "Just say, 'Peace be upon you.' '
n went on to say that in Montreal these days, "any Muslim girl who walks in the street can be abused." Her me
things were really not so bad. Both women wear a Muslim head covering, known as a hijab, which makes then
yn as a hijab, which makes them more visible than Muslim men. But, of course, when insults are directed at the

313 matches   Original text order   Strings matching: *Muslim*

863.90 kbytes, 1 file

Appendix J: Articles Used Pre-9/11 – Islam

	Date	Title	Writer
1.	August 10, 2001	An Islam Much Forgotten	Editorial Desk - Yossi Klein Halevi
2.	August 10, 2001	On Road to Endorsements by Ethnic Groups, Mayoral Hopefuls Fall Into Potholes	Jennifer Steinhauer
3.	August 10, 2001	Khatami vs. Khamenei	Editorial Desk
4.	August 10, 2001	Art in Review: The Holy Land Through the Eyes of Explorers	Grace Glueck
5.	August 13, 2001	MediaTalk; A Random Act of Survival in Jerusalem	Alex Kuczynski
6.	August 13, 2001	Bombing, and Shooting of Arab Girl Deepen Fear in Israel	Clyde Haberman
7.	August 13, 2001	Taliban Suspect Christian Plot Among Western Aid Workers	Associated Press
8.	August 16, 2001	Israelis Brandish Tanks as Threat; Kill Fatah Militiaman	Clyde Haberman
9.	August 16, 2001	Islam in Central Asia	Editorial Desk
10.	August 16, 2001	India Vows to Halt Terrorism Tied to Pakistan	Celia W. Dugger
11.	August 16, 2001	World Briefing Middle East: Egypt: Trial On Gay Charges Resumes	Reuters
12.	August 16, 2001	World Briefing Asia: Pakistan: Crackdown On Militants	Celia W. Dugger
13.	August 16, 2001	News Summary	NYT Staff
14.	August 19, 2001	Ali and the Ghosts of Manila	Letter to the Editor
15.	August 19, 2001	New Trial Set In Iran Killings Of Dissidents	Reuters
16.	August 22, 2001	Uzbek Crackdown	Letter to the Editor
17.	August 22, 2001	Explosion Wrecks a 14th-Century Monastery	Ian Fisher
18.	August 22, 2001	Dar es Salaam Journal; Tanzania Sees AIDS Lurking Between the Lines	Marc Lacey
19.	August 22, 2001	U.S. Seeking F.B.I.'s Return To Yemen, Says State Dept.	Reuters
20.	August 22, 2001	World Briefing Asia: Afghanistan: Thwarted Diplomats Leave	Barry Bearak
21.	August 22, 2001	World Briefing Middle East: Iran: Prison For Woman In Legislature	Agence France-Presse
22.	August 25, 2001	Jewish Collegians Prepare to Defend Israel on the Campuses	Jodi Wilgoren
23.	August 25, 2001	World Briefing Middle East: Saudi Arabia: Two More Beheadings	Associated Press
24.	August 28, 2001	2 Americans Allowed to See Their Jailed Daughters in Kabul	Barry Bearak
25.	August 31, 2001	New Delhi Journal; Modern India Gazes in Wonder at Its Gaudy Past	Celia W. Dugger
26.	August 31, 2001	Milosevic to Face Charges Covering 3 Wars in Balkans	Marlise Simons
27.	August 31, 2001	World Briefing Middle East: Afghanistan: Visit For Detained Australians	Reuters
28.	August 31, 2001	Technology Briefing Software: Suit Addresses	Associated Press

Appendix J: Articles Used Pre-9/11 – Islam		
Date	**Title**	**Writer**
	Offensive Chat	
29. September 6, 2001	Blasphemy in Pakistan	Letter to the Editor
30. September 6, 2001	Sri Lankan President Makes a Deal to Save Her Government	Celia W. Dugger
31. September 6, 2001	Israeli Party Is Bickering After Near-Tie In Its Primary	Clyde Haberman
32. September 9, 2001	Michael Mann and Will Smith in the Ring With Ali	Allen Barra
33. September 9, 2001	Following Up: A Son's Murder, A Mother's Nightmare	Joseph P. Fried
34. September 9, 2001	The Accord on Racism: The Objections; Crossfire Over Middle East and Slavery	Reuters
35. September 9, 2001	Accused Aid Workers Face Islamic Judges in Afghanistan	Barry Bearak
36. September 9, 2001	The Accord on Racism: The Declaration; Regrets for Past Wrongs & Hopes for Peace	NYT Staff
37. September 9, 2001	As Violence Rises in Mideast, Its People Sink Into Despair	Clyde Haberman
38. September 9, 2001	The New Season/Art: Pictures That Move, and Pop and Ping; Brazil, Past and Present	Holland Cotter
39. September 9, 2001	Love, Social Outrage and Is That a Whiff of Marijuana?	Bruce Weber
40. September 9, 2001	News Summary	NYT Staff

Appendix K: Articles Used Pre-9/11 – Muslim

	Date	Title	Writer
1.	August 10, 2001	An Islam Much Forgotten	Editorial Desk - Yossi Klein Halevi
2.	August 10, 2001	Political Memo; On Road to Endorsements by Ethnic Groups, Mayoral Hopefuls Fall Into Potholes	Jennifer Steinhauer
3.	August 10, 2001	Khatami vs. Khamenei	Editorial Desk
4.	August 10, 2001	World Briefing Europe: The Hague: Bosnians Plead Not Guilty	Agence France-Presse
5.	August 10, 2001	Art in Review; The Holy Land Through the Eyes of Explorers	Grace Glueck
6.	August 13, 2001	MediaTalk; A Random Act of Survival in Jerusalem	Alex Kuczynski
7.	August 13, 2001	Bombing, and Shooting of Arab Girl Deepen Fear in Israel	Clyde Haberman
8.	August 13, 2001	Taliban Suspect Christian Plot Among Western Aid Workers	Associated Press
9.	August 16, 2001	Israelis Brandish Tanks as Threat; Kill Fatah Militiaman	Clyde Haberman
10.	August 16, 2001	Islam in Central Asia	Editorial Desk
11.	August 16, 2001	India Vows to Halt Terrorism Tied to Pakistan	Celia W. Dugger
12.	August 16, 2001	World Briefing Europe: Bosnia: War-Crimes Suspect Surrenders	Associated Press
13.	August 16, 2001	World Briefing Middle East: Egypt: Trial On Gay Charges Resumes	Reuters
14.	August 16, 2001	World Briefing Asia: Pakistan: Crackdown On Militants	Celia W. Dugger
15.	August 19, 2001	Ali and the Ghosts of Manila	Letter to the Editor
16.	August 19, 2001	New Trial Set In Iran Killings Of Dissidents	Reuters
17.	August 22, 2001	Uzbek Crackdown	Letter to the Editor
18.	August 22, 2001	Explosion Wrecks a 14th-Century Monastery	Ian Fisher
19.	August 22, 2001	Dar es Salaam Journal; Tanzania Sees AIDS Lurking Between the Lines	Marc Lacey
20.	August 22, 2001	U.S. Seeking F.B.I.'s Return To Yemen, Says State Dept.	Reuters
21.	August 22, 2001	World Briefing Asia: Afghanistan: Thwarted Diplomats Leave	Barry Bearak
22.	August 22, 2001	World Briefing Middle East: Iran: Prison For Woman In Legislature	Agence France-Presse
23.	August 22, 2001	World Briefing Europe: Bosnia: Not Guilty, Bosnian Serb Says	Associated Press
24.	August 25, 2001	Jews in Hebron Only Wish That the Army Would Stay	Clyde Haberman
25.	August 25, 2001	Jewish Collegians Prepare to Defend Israel on the Campuses	Jodi Wilgoren
26.	August 25, 2001	World Briefing Middle East: Saudi Arabia: Two More Beheadings	Associated Press
27.	August 28, 2001	2 Americans Allowed to See Their Jailed Daughters	Barry Bearak

Appendix K: Articles Used Pre-9/11 – Muslim

Date	Title	Writer
	in Kabul	
28. August 31, 2001	New Delhi Journal; Modern India Gazes in Wonder at Its Gaudy Past	Celia W. Dugger
29. August 31, 2001	Milosevic to face charges covering 3 wars in Balkans	Marlise Simons
30. August 31, 2001	World Briefing Middle East: Afghanistan: Visit For Detained Australians	Reuters
31. August 31, 2001	Art Guide	NYT Staff
32. August 31, 2001	Technology Briefing Software: Suit Addresses Offensive Chat	Associated Press
33. September 6, 2001	Setting Out The Snares For Hackers	Jennifer Lee
34. September 6, 2001	Blasphemy in Pakistan	Letter to the Editor
35. September 6, 2001	Sri Lankan President Makes a Deal to Save Her Government	Celia W. Dugger
36. September 6, 2001	Essay; Sharon in Moscow	Editorial Desk – William Safire
37. September 9, 2001	Michael Mann and Will Smith in the Ring With Ali	Allen Barra
38. September 9, 2001	The Guide	Barbara Delatiner
39. September 9, 2001	Following Up: A Son's Murder, A Mother's Nightmare	Joseph P. Fried
40. September 9, 2001	Chinese Fight Crime With Torture and Executions	Craig S. Smith
41. September 9, 2001	The Accord on Racism: The Objections; Crossfire Over Middle East and Slavery	Reuters
42. September 9, 2001	Accused Aid Workers Face Islamic Judges in Afghanistan	Barry Bearak
43. September 9, 2001	The Accord on Racism: The Declaration; Regrets for Past Wrongs And Hopes for Peace	NYT Staff
44. September 9, 2001	As Violence Rises in Mideast, Its People Sink Into Despair	Clyde Haberman
45. September 9, 2001	Race Talks Finally Reach Accord On Slavery and Palestinian Plight	Rachel L. Swarns
46. September 9, 2001	The New Season/Art: Pictures That Move, and Pop and Ping: Brazil, Past and Present	Holland Cotter
47. September 9, 2001	News Summary	NYT Staff

Appendix L: Articles Used Post-9/11 – Islam

	Date	Title	Writer
1.	September 12, 2001	Religious and Ethnic Clashes in Nigeria Spread, Killing at Least 165	Reuters
2.	September 12, 2001	A Day of Terror: The Arabs; Condemnations From Arab Governments, but Widely Different Attitudes on the Street	Neil MacFarquhar
3.	September 12, 2001	A Day of Terror: The Afghans; Condemning Attacks, Taliban Says bin Laden Not Involved	Barry Bearak
4.	September 12, 2001	A Day of Terror: The Militant; America the Vulnerable Meets a Ruthless Enemy	John F. Burns
5.	September 12, 2001	Dispatches From a Day of Terror and Shock; U.S. Muslims' Pain	Letter to the Editor
6.	September 12, 2001	A Day of Terror: The Psychology; Attackers Believed To Be Sane	Erica Goode
7.	September 12, 2001	A Day of Terror: The Intelligence Agencies; Officials Say They Saw No Signs of Increased Terrorist Activity	James Risen & David Johnson
8.	September 12, 2001	A Day of Terror: The Ties; In U.S., Echoes of Rift Of Muslims and Jews	Laurie Goodstein
9.	September 12, 2001	Reaction From Around the World	NYT Staff, Reuters, Associated Press, Agence France-Presse
10.	September 16, 2001	Messing with Narnia	Letter to the Editor
11.	September 16, 2001	The Fragile City: Distance Has Totally Collapsed	Dalton Conley
12.	September 16, 2001	Before & After; Awakening to Terror, and Asking the World for Help	Joseph Kahn
13.	September 16, 2001	War Zone; What Would 'Victory' Mean?	Serge Schmemann
14.	September 16, 2001	This Time, The Scene Was Real	Neal Gabler
15.	September 16, 2001	After the Attacks: The Public; Poll Finds Strong Support for U.S. Use of Military Force	Richard L. Berke & Janet Elder
16.	September 16, 2001	After the Attacks: In Moscow; Russia Takes Stand Against Terrorism, but the Stance Wavers Quickly	Michael Wines
17.	September 16, 2001	After the Attacks: In Montreal; A Sense of Foreboding in Canada's Diverse Muslim Haven	Barbara Crossette
18.	September 16, 2001	After the Attacks: International Memo; America Inspires Both Longing and Loathing in Muslim World	John F. Burns
19.	September 16, 2001	After the Attacks: In Europe; A Pause To Ponder Washington's Tough Talk	Suzanne Daley
20.	September 16, 2001	After the Attacks: The Overview; Long Battle Seen	Elaine Sciolino
21.	September 16, 2001	After the Attacks: In Beijing; Waiting Nervously	Erik Eckholm

Date	Title	Writer
	Appendix L: Articles Used Post-9/11 – Islam	

Date	Title	Writer
	For Response	
22. September 16, 2001	After the Attacks: In Islamabad; Pakistan Antiterror Support Avoids Vow of Military Aid	John F. Burns
23. September 16, 2001	Sept. 9-15; Trial of Christians Continues	Barry Bearak
24. September 16, 2001	Weekend of Heartache: Let Us Honor the Dead; Paradox of Extremism	Letter to the Editor
25. September 16, 2001	Planning Counterattack	NYT Staff
26. September 16, 2001	After the Attacks	NYT Staff
27. September 20, 2001	Making Books; An Odd Business Felt Even Odder	Martin Arnold
28. September 20, 2001	Online Diary: Taking Refuge on the Internet, a Quilt of Tales and Solace	Pamela LiCalzi O'Connell
29. September 20, 2001	Close to Home: A Family Asks Why Together	Jay Heinrichs
30. September 20, 2001	Britain to Tighten Controls On Its Air and Sea Borders	Alan Cowell
31. September 20, 2001	Mideast Truce Holds, With Scattered Violence	Ian Fisher
32. September 20, 2001	Europe Moves To Toughen Laws to Fight Terrorism	Donald G. McNeil, Jr.
33. September 20, 2001	Essay; Equal Time for Hitler?	Editorial Desk - William Safire
34. September 20, 2001	A Nation Challenged: The Neighbor; Pakistani Defends Joining with U.S.	John F. Burns
35. September 20, 2001	Metro Matters; Our Daily Tribute to Differences Provokes Dislike Among Many	Joyce Purnick
36. September 20, 2001	In a Wounded Land, the Drums of September; Taunted and Threatened	Letter to the editor
37. September 20, 2001	Metro Briefing Connecticut: Hartford: Anti-Bias Group Formed	Associated Press
38. September 24, 2001	A Nation Challenge: The Energy Market; Military Plans Must Ensure Oil Flow	Neela Banerjee
39. September 24, 2001	A Familiar Anguish Revisited	Mirta Orjito
40. September 24, 2001	Hamas Signals Suspension of Suicide Bombings	Joel Greenberg
41. September 24, 2001	TV Sports; Long-Needed Perspective On the Air	Richard Sandomir
42. September 24, 2001	Essay; The Ultimate Enemy	Editorial Desk – William Safire
43. September 24, 2001	A Nation Challenged: The Papal Trip; Pope, in Central Asia, Speaks Out Against Any Overzealous Military Response by the U.S.	Melinda Henneberger
44. September 24, 2001	Finances of Terror	Editorial Desk
45. September 24, 2001	A Nation Challenged: Gulf Allies; Six Arab States Offer Support	Warren Hoge
46. September 24, 2001	A Nation Challenged: Arab Ally; Saudis Feeling Pain of Supporting U.S.	Patrick E. Tyler
47. September 24, 2001	In America; Leading America Beyond Fear	Editorial Desk – Bob Herbert
48. September 24, 2001	A Nation Challenged: Heir Apparent; Egyptian Seen As Top Aide And Successor To bin	Douglas Jehl

Appendix L: Articles Used Post-9/11 – Islam

Date	Title	Writer
	Laden	
49. September 24, 2001	A Nation Challenged: Cabbies; Drivers Say They Risk Violence by Working, and May Even Lose Money	Randy Kennedy
50. September 24, 2001	The Awakened Giant: How Will It Strike Back?	Letter to the Editor
51. September 24, 2001	The Awakened Giant: How Will It Strike Back?	Letter to the Editor
52. September 24, 2001	A Nation Challenged: The Region; End of Sanctions May Ease Pakistanis' Despair Even as the Afghans' Grows Worse	John F. Burns
53. September 24, 2001	The Awakened Giant: How Will It Strike Back?; The Faces of America	Letter to the Editor
54. September 24, 2001	A Nation Challenged: The Strategy; U.S. Seeks Afghan Coalition Against Taliban	Michael R. Gordon & Eric Schmitt
55. September 24, 2001	A Nation Challenged: Visiting Briton to Meet Iranian Leaders	Agence France-Presse
56. September 24, 2001	A Nation Challenged: Arab Americans; A Request For Patience If the Law Overreaches	David M. Halbfinger
57. September 24, 2001	A Nation Challenged: The Proof; U.S. to Publish Terror Evidence On bin Laden	Jane Perlez & Tim Weiner
58. September 28, 2001	Film Review; Married but Seldom With a Husband	Stephen Holden
59. September 28, 2001	Past Recalled for Japanese-Americans	Evelyn Nieves
60. September 28, 2001	Finding Allies in a World of Shadows	Martin Indyk
61. September 28, 2001	Furor at Berlusconi Remark on West's Superiority	NYT Staff
62. September 28, 2001	A Nation Challenged: Jakarta; U.S. Lets Employees Leave As Indonesia Protests Mount	Seth Mydans
63. September 28, 2001	Year of Intifada Sees Hardening on Each Side	James Bennet
64. September 28, 2001	A Nation Challenged: The Emissary; Jesse Jackson Says He Might Go to Taliban to Seek Turnaround	Raymond Hernandez
65. September 28, 2001	Pop Star and Public Officials Join Campaign for Tolerance	Susan Sachs
66. September 28, 2001	A Nation Challenged: Choice of Words; In a Military Town, Osama's Place Cafe Is Tasting Tolerance	Stephen Kinzer
67. September 28, 2001	Many Paths to Action, in New York and the World	Letter to the Editor
68. September 28, 2001	A Nation Challenged: The Lawyer; Defending Muslims in Court And Drawing Death Threats As Well as a High Profile	William Glaberson
69. September 28, 2001	A Nation Challenged: Prisoners; Taliban Enlisting Eager Recruits of Many Lands	David Rohde
70. September 28, 2001	A Nation Challenged: The Hunted; New Push to Get bin Laden To Agree to Quit Afghanistan	John F. Burns
71. September 28, 2001	Radio Messages On Tolerance	NYT Staff
72. September 28, 2001	News Summary	NYT Staff

	Appendix L: Articles Used Post-9/11 – Islam	
Date	**Title**	**Writer**
73. October 2, 2001	MTV, Turning Serious, Helps Its Generation Cope	Jim Rutenberg
74. October 2, 2001	Foreign Affairs; Eastern Middle School	Thomas L. Friedman
75. October 2, 2001	New Fears, New Alliance	Editorial Desk - Edward N. Luttwak
76. October 2, 2001	A Sense of American Unfairness Erodes Support in Gulf States	Warren Hoge
77. October 2, 2001	Supreme Court Roundup; In a New Term's Somber First Day, Justices Hear Arguments on Inmate Rights	Linda Greenhouse
78. October 2, 2001	America's Central Asian Allies	Editorial Desk
79. October 2, 2001	A Nation Challenged: The Afghan Opposition; Ex-King and Rebels to Hold Special Council	Melinda Henneberger
80. October 2, 2001	A Nation Challenged: The Soldiers; 12-Year-Olds Take Up Arms Against Taliban	David Rohde
81. October 2, 2001	Before Attacks, U.S. Was Ready To Say It Backed Palestinian State	Jane Perlez & Patrick E. Tyler
82. October 2, 2001	A Nation Challenged: News Analysis; In Pakistan, A Shaky Ally	Barry Bearak
83. October 2, 2001	A Nation Challenged: The Fleet; Pentagon Dispatches 3rd Carrier Toward Gulf	Steven L. Myers & Eric Schmitt
84. October 2, 2001	A Nation Challenged: Islamabad; Pakistani Leader Now Expects U.S. Military Action	John F. Burns
85. October 2, 2001	A Nation Challenged: Repercussion; 26 Die as Suicide Squad Bombs Kashmir Legislative Building	Barry Bearak
86. October 2, 2001	The Fight Ahead: Can We Learn From the Past?; The Muslim Clerics	Letter to the Editor
87. October 2, 2001	The Fight Ahead: Can We Learn From the Past?; The Muslim Clerics	Letter to the Editor
88. October 2, 2001	A Nation Challenged: The Money; 19 Countries Vow to Seize Bank Assets Of Terrorists	Joseph Kahn
89. October 2, 2001	The Fight Ahead: Can We Learn From the Past?; Ideas for the Site	Letter to the Editor
90. October 2, 2001	A Nation Challenged: Bosnia; NATO Says 4 Arrested Near Sarajevo Are Suspected of Terror Activities	Carlotta Gall
91. October 2, 2001	World Briefing Europe: Italy: Berlusconi Seeks To Make Amends	Marina Harss
92. October 2, 2001	National Briefing South: Louisiana: Ruling Against School's Bible Program	Associated Press
93. October 2, 2001	A Nation Challenged: The President; Bush Expected to Give Approval To Airport's Reopening Shortly	Elisabeth Bumiller
94. October 2, 2001	A Nation Challenged: Land of Fear; Afghanistan's Ethnic Groups, and Pinpointing the Taliban's Strongpoints	NYT Staff
95. October 6, 2001	Muslim Rebels Raid Town in Southern	Agence France-Presse

Appendix L: Articles Used Post-9/11 – Islam

Date	Title	Writer
	Philippines	
96. October 6, 2001	The Case Against bin Laden	Editorial Desk
97. October 6, 2001	A Prayer Before Flying; Places to Worship Help Soothe Souls at an Airport	Sarah Kershaw
98. October 6, 2001	A Nation Challenged: Protesters; A Pro-Taliban Rally Draws Angry Thousands in Pakistan, Then Melts Away	Rick Bragg
99. October 6, 2001	A Nation Challenged: Islamabad; In Pakistan, Blair Repeats Allies' Goals	John F. Burns
100. October 6, 2001	A Nation Challenged: Fort Drum, N.Y.; U.S. Troops Are Deployed To Former U.S.S.R.	Richard Perez-Pena
101. October 6, 2001	A Nation Challenged: Muslims and the Military; Ties Between a Mosque and Fort Bragg Stay Strong and Neighborly	Gustav Niebuhr
102. October 6, 2001	A Nation Challenged: Conflict Views; On Streets Of Jordan, Doubts Lurk About War	Ian Fisher
103. October 6, 2001	Bangladesh to Swear In Leader on Monday	Associated Press
104. October 6, 2001	Slain Arab-American May Have Been Hate-Crime Victim	Evelyn Nieves
105. October 6, 2001	A Nation Challenged: The Media; Islam and Its Adherents Ride the Publicity Wave	Caryn James
106. October 6, 2001	A Nation Challenged: Frustrated Ally; Raising Munich, Sharon Reveals Israeli Qualms	Serge Schmemann
107. October 6, 2001	A Nation Challenged: The Flight Instructor; Algerian Pilot Held in London Was Hijacking Suspects' Lead Trainer, Prosecutor Says	Anthony DePalma w/ Raymond Bonner
108. October 6, 2001	A Nation Challenged: Preparing for War; U.S. and Britain Make Late Push to Forge Coalition for Combat	David E. Sanger w/ Michael R. Gordon
109. October 6, 2001	U.S. and Afghans: Decision Time	Letter to the Editor
110. October 6, 2001	A Nation Challenged: Strategy; Taliban's Rivals Show off Forces	David Rohde
111. October 6, 2001	A Nation Challenged: The Suspects; F.B.I. Curbed Scrutiny of Man Now a Suspect in the Attacks	David Johnston & Philip Shenon
112. October 6, 2001	Public Lives: In Nebraska, an Oasis of Insight Into Afghanistan's Heart	Jodi Wilgoren
113. October 6, 2001	A Nation Challenged: An Overview: OCT. 5, 2001; A Nod From the Uzbeks, Coalition-Building and Sharon's Angry Words	Clyde Haberman
114. October 6, 2001	A Nation Challenged	NYT Staff
115. October 10, 2001	Management: Contingency Plans to Fill Reservists' Shoes	Maggie Jackson
116. October 10, 2001	Oil Companies Are Increasing Their Already Tight Security	Neela Banerjee
117. October 10, 2001	Lynne Cheney Disputes Official's Call for More Teaching of Multiculturalism	Anemona Hartocollis

Appendix L: Articles Used Post-9/11 – Islam

Date	Title	Writer
118. October 10, 2001	A Nation Challenged: Street Rage; Pakistani Police Kill 3 Protesters and a 13-Year-Old	Douglas Frantz
119. October 10, 2001	A Nation Challenged: The Region; 5 Ex-Soviet Asian Republics Are Now Courted by the U.S.	Stephen Kinzer
120. October 10, 2001	A Nation Challenged: Uzbekistan; The Signs Of a Buildup Are Becoming More Evident	C. J. Chivers
121. October 10, 2001	Widening Gap: Arafat Struggles to Control Hamas	James Bennet
122. October 10, 2001	A Nation Challenged: The President; The U.S.-Pakistan Relationship Shows the First Sign of Tension	David E. Sanger
123. October 10, 2001	A Nation Challenged: The Rulers; America's Muslim Allies: A Time of Trial	John Kifner
124. October 10, 2001	A Nation Challenged: Tehran; The Iranians Seek to Stem Refugee Flow	Nazila Fathi
125. October 10, 2001	A Nation Challenged:The Fighting;Pakistan, in a Border Clash, Turns Back Taliban Forces	John F. Burns
126. October 6, 2001	A Nation Challenged: Indonesia; Anti-American Protests Increase, and Sponsors Plan More	Seth Mydans
127. October 6, 2001	A Nation Challenged: United Nations; U.S. Ambassador Warns Iraq Against Stirring Up Trouble	Serge Schmemann
128. October 6, 2001	A Nation Challenged: The Mastermind; A Portrait of the Terrorist: From Shy Child to Single-Minded Killer	Jim Yardley
129. October 6, 2001	A Nation Challenged: Relations; Sept. 11 Attack Narrows the Racial Divide	Somini Sengupta
130. October 6, 2001	Censorship in Pashto and Arabic	Editorial Desk
131. October 6, 2001	A Nation Challenged: The Networks – Critic's Notebook; A Public Flooded With Images From Friend and Foe Alike	Caryn James
132. October 6, 2001	A Nation Challenged: The Videotape; Bin Laden Aide Threatens More Strikes	John F. Burns
133. October 6, 2001	A Nation Challenged: North of Kabul; Armed Adversaries Maintaining Fragile Radio Contacts Across the Front Line	David Rohde
134. October 6, 2001	A Nation Challenged: The Damage; Pentagon Says Bombs Destroy Terror Camps	Judith Miller
135. October 6, 2001	India, Upset by Kashmir, Rejects 2nd Pakistan Invitation	Celia W. Dugger
136. October 6, 2001	A Nation Challenged: The Pentagon; U.S. Said to Plan Copter Raids in Afghanistan	Steven Lee Myers
137. October 6, 2001	A Nation Challenged: Global Links; Other Fronts Seen	Tim Weiner
138. October 6, 2001	National Briefing Rockies: Wyoming: Delay In Trial Of Pakistani	Michael Janofsky

Appendix L: Articles Used Post-9/11 – Islam		
Date	**Title**	**Writer**
139. October 6, 2001	News Summary	NYT Staff

Appendix M: Articles Used Post-9/11 – Muslim

	Date	Title	Writer
1.	September 12, 2001	Religious and Ethnic Clashes in Nigeria Spread, Killing at Least 165	Reuters
2.	September 12, 2001	A Day of Terror: The Arabs; Condemnations From Arab Governments, but Widely Different Attitudes on the Street	Neil MacFarquhar
3.	September 12, 2001	A Day of Terror: The Afghans; Condemning Attacks, Taliban Says bin Laden Not Involved	Barry Bearak
4.	September 12, 2001	A Day of Terror: The Militants; America the Vulnerable Meets a Ruthless Enemy	John F. Burns
5.	September 12, 2001	Dispatches From a Day of Terror and Shock; U.S. Muslims' Pain	Letter to the Editor
6.	September 12, 2001	A Day of Terror: The Psychology; Attackers Believed To Be Sane	Erica Goode
7.	September 12, 2001	A Day of Terror: Intelligence Agencies; Officials Say They Saw No Signs of Increased Terrorist Activity	James Risen & David Johnston
8.	September 12, 2001	A Day of Terror: The Ties; In U.S., Echoes of Rift Of Muslims and Jews	Laurie Goodstein
9.	September 16, 2001	Messing With Narnia	Letter to the Editor
10.	September 16, 2001	Five Questions for Kerry J. Sulkowicz; As Many Ways to Grieve as There Are Desks in the Office	Jonathan D. Glater
11.	September 16, 2001	The Fragile City: Distance Has Totally Collapsed	Dalton Conley
12.	September 16, 2001	Fighting an Elusive Enemy	David M. Kennedy
13.	September 16, 2001	Before & After; Awakening to Terror, and Asking the World for Help	Joseph Kahn
14.	September 16, 2001	War Zone: What Price Liberty?; The Clamor Of a Free People	Linda Greenhouse
15.	September 16, 2001	War Zone; What Would 'Victory' Mean?	Serge Schmemann
16.	September 16, 2001	This Time, The Scene Was Real	Neal Gabler
17.	September 16, 2001	After the Attacks: The Public; Poll Finds Strong Support for U.S. Use of Military Force	Richard L. Berke & Janet Elder
18.	September 16, 2001	After the Attacks: In Moscow; Russia Takes Stand Against Terrorism, but the Stance Wavers Quickly	Michael Wines
19.	September 16, 2001	After the Attacks: In Montreal; A Sense of Foreboding in Canada's Diverse Muslim Haven	Barbara Crossette
20.	September 16, 2001	After the Attacks: International Memo; America Inspires Both Longing and Loathing in Muslim World	John F. Burns
21.	September 16, 2001	After the Attacks: In Europe; A Pause To Ponder Washington's Tough Talk	Suzanne Daley
22.	September 16, 2001	Taliban Opposition Confirms Death of Its Battle	Barry Bearak

Appendix M: Articles Used Post-9/11 – Muslim

Date	Title	Writer
	Commander	
23. September 16, 2001	After the Attacks: The Overview; Long Battle	Elaine Sciolino
24. September 16, 2001	After the Attacks: In Beijing; Waiting Nervously For Response	Erik Eckholm
25. September 16, 2001	After the Attacks: In Islamabad; Pakistan Antiterror Support Avoids Vow of Military Aid	John F. Burns
26. September 16, 2001	Sept. 9-15; Trial of Christians Continues	Barry Bearak
27. September 16, 2001	After the Attacks: The Organization; Old War Escalates on a New Front: The Trail of Relentless Martyrs	Judith Miller
28. September 16, 2001	Weekend of Heartache: Let Us Honor the Dead; Paradox of Extremism	Letter to the Editor
29. September 16, 2001	Cape Town	Michael Mewshaw
30. September 16, 2001	In This Section	NYT Staff
31. September 20, 2001	Online Diary: Taking Refuge on the Internet, a Quilt of Tales and Solace	Pamela LiCalzi O'Connell
32. September 20, 2001	The War on Terror Is Not New	Niall Ferguson
33. September 20, 2001	Britain to Tighten Controls On Its Air and Sea Borders	Alan Cowell
34. September 20, 2001	Mideast Truce Holds, With Scattered Violence	Ian Fisher
35. September 20, 2001	Europe Moves To Toughen Laws to Fight Terrorism	Donald G. McNeil, Jr.
36. September 20, 2001	Essay; Equal Time for Hitler?	Editorial Desk – William Safire
37. September 20, 2001	A Nation Challenged: The Allies; NATO, Though Supportive, Has Little to Offer Militarily	Suzanne Daley
38. September 20, 2001	A Nation Challenged: The Neighbor; Pakistani Defends Joining with U.S.	John F. Burns
39. September 20, 2001	Metro Matters; Our Daily Tribute to Differences Provokes Dislike Among Many	Joyce Purnick
40. September 20, 2001	A Nation Challenged: The Investigation; 3 Held in Detroit After Aircraft Diagrams Are Found	David Johnston w/ Paul Zielbauer
41. September 20, 2001	In a Wounded Land, the Drums of September; Taunted and Threatened	Letter to the Editor
42. September 20, 2001	A Nation Challenged: The Overview; Bush Orders Heavy Bombers Near Afghans; Demands bin Laden Now, Not Negotiating	David E. Sanger
43. September 20, 2001	Metro Briefing Connecticut: Hartford: Anti-Bias Group Formed	Associated Press
44. September 20, 2001	World Briefing Europe: Bosnia And Herzegovina: Plea Bargain By Serb	Associated Press
45. September 24, 2001	A Nation Challenged: The Energy Market; Military Plans Must Ensure Oil Flow	Neela Banerjee
46. September 24, 2001	A Swift and United Response From Entertainers	Bernard Weinraub & Neil Strauss

Appendix M: Articles Used Post-9/11 – Muslim

Date	Title	Writer
47. September 24, 2001	A Nation Challenged: The Journalists; Terror Experts Use Lenses of Their Specialties	Felicity Barringer
48. September 24, 2001	A Familiar Anguish Revisited	Mirta Ojito
49. September 24, 2001	Hamas Signals Suspension of Suicide Bombings	Joel Greenberg
50. September 24, 2001	Essay; The Ultimate Enemy	Editorial Desk – William Safire
51. September 24, 2001	A Nation Challenged: The Papal Trip; Pope, in Central Asia, Speaks Out Against Any Overzealous Military Response by the U.S.	Melinda Henneberger
52. September 24, 2001	Finances of Terror	Editorial Desk
53. September 24, 2001	A Nation Challenged: Gulf Allies; Six Arab States Offer Support	Warren Hoge
54. September 24, 2001	A Nation Challenged: Arab Ally; Saudis Feeling Pain of Supporting U.S.	Patrick E. Tyler
55. September 24, 2001	In America; Leading America Beyond Fear	Bob Herbert
56. September 24, 2001	Primary Candidates Urge Voters to Turn Out as an Act of Defiance	Adam Nagourney
57. September 24, 2001	A Nation Challenged: Heir Apparent; Egyptian Seen As Top Aide And Successor To bin Laden	Douglas Jehl
58. September 24, 2001	A Nation Challenged: Cabbies; Drivers Say They Risk Violence by Working, and May Even Lose Money	Randy Kennedy
59. September 24, 2001	The Awakened Giant: How Will It Strike Back?	Letter to the Editor
60. September 24, 2001	The Awakened Giant: How Will It Strike Back?	Letter to the Editor
61. September 24, 2001	A Nation Challenged: The Region; End of Sanctions May Ease Pakistanis' Despair Even as the Afghans' Grows Worse	John F. Burns
62. September 24, 2001	The Awakened Giant: How Will It Strike Back?; The Faces of America	Letter to the Editor
63. September 24, 2001	A Nation Challenged: The Strategy; U.S. Seeks Afghan Coalition Against Taliban	Michael R. Gordon & Eric Schmitt
64. September 24, 2001	Victims of '93 Bombay Terror Wary of U.S. Motives	Celia W. Dugger
65. September 24, 2001	A Nation Challenged: Visiting Briton to Meet Iranian Leaders	Agence France-Presse
66. September 24, 2001	A Nation Challenged: Arab-Americans; A Request For Patience If the Law Overreaches	David M. Halbfinger
67. September 24, 2001	A Nation Challenged: The Service; In a Stadium of Heroes, Prayers for the Fallen and Solace for Those Left Behind	Robert D. McFadden
68. September 24, 2001	A Nation Challenged: The Proof; U.S. to Publish Terror Evidence On bin Laden	Jane Perlez & Tim Weiner
69. September 24, 2001	Metro Briefing Connecticut: Hartford: Ministers Plan Muslim Safe House	Associated Press
70. September 24, 2001	A Nation Challenged	NYT Staff
71. September 28, 2001	Film Review; Married but Seldom With a Husband	Stephen Holden

Appendix M: Articles Used Post-9/11 – Muslim

Date	Title	Writer
72. September 28, 2001	Photography Review; Capturing the Serenity Where Turmoil Reigns	Margarett Loke
73. September 28, 2001	Asia Casts a Wary Eye to the West	Mark Landler
74. September 28, 2001	Past Recalled for Japanese-Americans	Evelyn Nieves
75. September 28, 2001	Finding Allies in a World of Shadows	Editorial Desk – Martin Indyk
76. September 28, 2001	Furor at Berlusconi Remark on West's Superiority	NYT Staff
77. September 28, 2001	A Nation Challenged: Jakarta; U.S. Lets Employees Leave As Indonesia Protests Mount	Seth Mydans
78. September 28, 2001	Year of Intifada Sees Hardening on Each Side	James Bennet
79. September 28, 2001	A Nation Challenged: The Emissary; Jesse Jackson Says He Might Go to Taliban to Seek Turnaround	Raymond Hernandez
80. September 28, 2001	Pop Star and Public Officials Join Campaign for Tolerance	Susan Sachs
81. September 28, 2001	A Nation Challenged: Choice of Words; In a Military Town, Osama's Place Cafe Is Tasting Tolerance	Stephen Kinzer
82. September 28, 2001	Many Paths to Action, in New York and the World	Letter to the Editor
83. September 28, 2001	A Nation Challenged: The Lawyer; Defending Muslims in Court And Drawing Death Threats As Well as a High Profile	William Glaberson
84. September 28, 2001	A Nation Challenged: Prisoners; Taliban Enlisting Eager Recruits of Many Lands	David Rohde
85. September 28, 2001	A Nation Challenged: The Hunted; New Push to Get bin Laden To Agree to Quit Afghanistan	John F. Burns
86. September 28, 2001	Radio Messages On Tolerance	NYT Staff
87. September 28, 2001	News Summary	NYT STaff
88. October 2, 2001	Arts in America; When Afghanistan Collapsed	Sarah Boxer
89. October 2, 2001	MTV, Turning Serious, Helps Its Generation Cope	Jim Rutenberg
90. October 2, 2001	Foreign Affairs; Eastern Middle School	Editorial Desk – Thomas L.Friedman
91. October 2, 2001	New Fears, New Alliance	Editorial Desk – Edward N. Luttwak
92. October 2, 2001	A Sense of American Unfairness Erodes Support in Gulf States	Warren Hoge
93. October 2, 2001	Supreme Court Roundup; In a New Term's Somber First Day, Justices Hear Arguments on Inmate Rights	Linda Greenhouse
94. October 2, 2001	America's Central Asian Allies	Editorial Desk
95. October 2, 2001	A Nation Challenged: The Afghan Opposition; Ex-King and Rebels to Hold Special Council	Melinda Henneberger
96. October 2, 2001	A Nation Challenged: The Soldiers; 12-Year-Olds Take Up Arms Against Taliban	David Rohde
97. October 2, 2001	Before Attacks, U.S. Was Ready To Say It Backed Palestinian State	Jane Perlez & Patrick E. Tyler

Appendix M: Articles Used Post-9/11 – Muslim

Date	Title	Writer
98. October 2, 2001	A Nation Challenged: News Analysis; In Pakistan, A Shaky Ally	Barry Bearak
99. October 2, 2001	A Nation Challenged: The Mayor; Giuliani is Blunt in Rare U.N. Talk	Serge Schmemann
100. October 2, 2001	A Nation Challenged: Islamabad; Pakistani Leader Now Expects U.S. Military Action	John F. Burns
101. October 2, 2001	A Nation Challenged: Repercussions; 26 Die as Suicide Squad Bombs Kashmir Legislative Building	Barry Bearak
102. October 2, 2001	The Fight Ahead: Can We Learn From the Past?; The Muslim Clerics	Letter to the Editor
103. October 2, 2001	The Fight Ahead: Can We Learn From the Past?; The Muslim Clerics	Letter to the Editor
104. October 2, 2001	A Nation Challenged: The Money; 19 Countries Vow to Seize Bank Assets Of Terrorists	Joseph Kahn
105. October 2, 2001	The Fight Ahead: Can We Learn From the Past?; The Radical Lawyer	Letter to the Editor
106. October 2, 2001	The Fight Ahead: Can We Learn From the Past?; Ideas for the Site	Letter to the Editor
107. October 2, 2001	A Nation Challenged: Bosnia; NATO Says 4 Arrested Near Sarajevo Are Suspected of Terror Activities	Carlotta Gall
108. October 2, 2001	World Briefing Europe: Italy: Berlusconi Seeks To Make Amends	Marina Harss
109. October 2, 2001	National Briefing South: Louisiana: Ruling Against School's Bible Program	Associated Press
110. October 6, 2001	Counterpoint to Unity: Dissent	Richard Bernstein
111. October 6, 2001	A Year Later, Free Serbia Struggles to Overcome Its Past	Carlotta Gall
112. October 6, 2001	Muslim Rebels Raid Town in Southern Philippines	Agence France-Presse
113. October 6, 2001	Correspondent; The 40-Year War	Bill Keller
114. October 6, 2001	Immigrant Who Didn't Understand Robber Is Killed	Robert Lezin Jones
115. October 6, 2001	The Case Against bin Laden	Editorial Desk
116. October 6, 2001	A Prayer Before Flying; Places to Worship Help Soothe Souls at an Airport	Sarah Kershaw
117. October 6, 2001	A Nation Challenged: Protesters; A Pro-Taliban Rally Draws Angry Thousands in Pakistan, Then Melts Away	Rick Bragg
118. October 6, 2001	A Nation Challenged: Islamabad; In Pakistan, Blair Repeats Allies' Goals	John F. Burns
119. October 6, 2001	A Nation Challenged: Fort Drum, N.Y.; U.S. Troops Are Deployed To Former U.S.S.R.	Richard Perez-Pena
120. October 6, 2001	A Nation Challenged: Muslims and the Military; Ties Between a Mosque and Fort Bragg Stay Strong and Neighborly	Gustav Niebuhr
121. October 6, 2001	A Nation Challenged: Conflicting Views;	Ian Fisher

Appendix M: Articles Used Post-9/11 – Muslim

Date	Title	Writer
	On Streets Of Jordan, Doubts Lurk About War	
122. October 6, 2001	Bangladesh to Swear In Leader on Monday	Associated Press
123. October 6, 2001	Slain Arab-American May Have Been Hate-Crime Victim	Evelyn Nieves
124. October 6, 2001	A Nation Challenged: The Media; Islam and Its Adherents Ride the Publicity Wave	Caryn James
125. October 6, 2001	A Nation Challenged: Frustrated Ally; Raising Munich, Sharon Reveals Israeli Qualms	Serge Schmemann
126. October 6, 2001	A Nation Challenged: The Rift; U.S. Strongly Rebukes Sharon for Criticism of Bush, Calling It 'Unacceptable'	Jane Perlez & Katharine Q. Seelye
127. October 6, 2001	A Nation Challenged: The Flight Instructor; Algerian Pilot Held in London Was Hijacking Suspects' Lead Trainer, Prosecutor Says	Anthony DePalma, w/ Raymond Bonner
128. October 6, 2001	A Nation Challenged: Preparing for War; U.S. and Britain Make Late Push to Forge Coalition for Combat	David E. Sanger, w/ Michael R. Gordon
129. October 6, 2001	U.S. and Afghans: Decision Time	Letter to the Editor
130. October 6, 2001	A Nation Challenged: Strategy; Taliban's Rivals Show Off Forces	David Rohde
131. October 6, 2001	A Nation Challenged: The Evidence; White House Approved Data Blair Released	David E. Sanger
132. October 6, 2001	A Nation Challenged: The Suspects; F.B.I. Curbed Security of Man Now a Suspect in the Attacks	David Johnston & Philip Shenon
133. October 6, 2001	Public Lives: In Nebraska, an Oasis of Insight Into Afghanistan's Heart	Jodi Wilgoren
134. October 6, 2001	News Summary	NYT Staff
135. October 6, 2001	A Nation Challenged: An Overview: Oct. 5, 2001; A Nod From the Uzbeks, Coalition-Building and Sharon's Angry Words	Clyde Haberman
136. October 10, 2001	The Balancing Act That Is Thai, Salads Not Excepted	Eric Asimov
137. October 10, 2001	The Laugh Lab at Carnegie Hall	Peter Marks
138. October 10, 2001	Lynne Cheney Disputes Official's Call for More Teaching of Multiculturalism	Anemona Hartocollis
139. October 10, 2001	A Nation Challenged: Street Rage; Pakistani Police Kill 3 Protesters and a 13-Year-Old	Douglas Frantz
140. October 10, 2001	A Nation Challenged: The Reason; 5 Ex-Soviet Asian Republics Are Now Courted by the U.S.	Stephen Kinzer
141. October 10, 2001	A Nation Challenged: Uzbekistan; The Signs Of a Buildup Are Becoming More Evident	C. J. Chivers
142. October 10, 2001	Widening Gap: Arafat Struggles to Control Hamas	James Bennet
143. October 10, 2001	A Nation Challenged: The President; The U.S.-Pakistan Relationship Shows the First	David E. Sanger

Date	Title	Writer
	Appendix M: Articles Used Post-9/11 – Muslim	
	Sign of Tension	
144. October 10, 2001	A Nation Challenged: The Rulers; America's Muslim Allies: A Time of Trial	John Kifner
145. October 10, 2001	A Nation Challenged: Tehran; The Iranians Seek to Stem Refugee Flow	Nazila Fathi
146. October 10, 2001	A Nation Challenged: The Fighting; Pakistan, in a Border Clash, Turns Back Taliban Forces	John F. Burns
147. October 10, 2001	A Nation Challenged: Indonesia; Anti-American Protests Increase, and Sponsors Plan More	Seth Mydans
148. October 10, 2001	A Nation Challenged: United Nations; U.S. Ambassador Warns Iraq Against Stirring Up Trouble	Serge Schmemann
149. October 10, 2001	A Nation Challenged: The Mastermind; A Portrait of the Terrorist: From Shy Child to Single-Minded Killer	Jim Yardley
150. October 10, 2001	A Nation Challenged: Relations; Sept. 11 Attack Narrows the Racial Divide	Somini Sengupta
151. October 10, 2001	Censorship in Pashto and Arabic	Letter to the Editor
152. October 10, 2001	A Nation Challenged: The Isolated Town; Faraway Events Hit Home For Town in Eastern Oregon	Timothy Egan
153. October 10, 2001	A Nation Challenged: The Networks – Critic's Notebook; A Public Flooded With Images From Friend and Foe Alike	Caryn James
154. October 10, 2001	A Nation Challenged: The Videotape; Bin Laden Aide Threatens More Strikes	John F. Burns
155. October 10, 2001	A Nation Challenged: North of Kabul; Armed Adversaries Maintaining Fragile Radio Contacts Across the Front Line	David Rohde
156. October 10, 2001	A Nation Challenged: The Damage; Pentagon Says Bombs Destroy Terror Camps	Judith Miller
157. October 10, 2001	India, Upset by Kashmir, Rejects 2nd Pakistan Invitation	Celia W. Dugger
158. October 10, 2001	A Nation Challenged: Casualties; U.S. Raids Kill 4 U.N. Aides Outside Kabul	Barry Bearak
159. October 10, 2001	A Nation Challenged: Global Links; Other Fronts Seen	Tom Weiner
160. October 10, 2001	National Briefing Rockies: Wyoming: Delay In Trial Of Pakistani	Michael Janofsky

Works Cited

American Heritage Dictionary of the English Language (4th Ed.). (n.d.) Retrieved April 10, 2007 from Answers.com: http://www.answers.com/topic/hard-news

Ashley, L., & Olson, B. (1998). Constructing reality: Print media's framing of the women's movement. *Journalism & Mass Communication Quarterly, 75,* 263-277.

Barlow, M. (2003). *Concordancing and corpus analysis using MP 2.2.* Houston, TX: Athelstan.

Bearak, B. (2001, October 2). In Pakistan, a shaky ally. *The New York Times*, pp. 1.

Berger, A.A. (1995). *Essentials of mass communication theory*. Thousand Oaks, California, Sage Publications, Inc.

Bracci, S.L. (2003). Ethical issues in media production. In A.N. Valdivia (Ed.), *A companion to media studies* (pp. 115-136). Malden, MA: Blackwell Publishing, Ltd.

Brewer, P., Aday, S., & Gross, K. (2003). Rallies all around: The dynamics of system support. . In P. Norris, M. Kern, & M. Just (Eds.), *Framing terrorism* (pp. 229-253). London, Great Britain: Routledge.

Burns, J.F. (2001, September 16). Pakistan anti-terror support avoids vow of military aid. *The New York Times*, pp. 5.

Council on American-Islamic Relations. (2004, August). *Islam and Muslims: A poll of American public opinion.* Retrieved on April 25, 2007 from: http://www.cair-net.org/downloads/pollresults.ppt#256

Cohen, B. (1963). *The press and foreign policy.* Princeton, N.J: Princeton University Press.

Davidson, L. (2003). Al-Jazeera: How the free Arab news network scooped the world and changed the Middle East. *Middle East Policy, 10*(1), 172-76.

El-Nawawy, M., & Iskandar, A. (2003). *Al-Jazeera: The story of the network that is rattling governments and redefining modern journalism*. Denver, CO: Westview Press.

Entman, R. (1993). Framing: Toward clarification of a fractured paradigm. *Journal of Communication, 43*, 51–58.

Fisher, W. (March 1984). Narration as a human communication paradigm: The case of public moral argument. *Communication Monographs, 51*, 1-22.

Ford, P. (2001, September 19). Europe cringes at Bush 'crusade' against terrorists. The *Christian Science Monitor.* Retrieved on April 12, 2007 from http://www.csmonitor.com/2001/0919/p12s2-woeu.html

Gallup International. (2003). *Gallup International Iraq Poll 2003.* Retrieved on April 10, 2007 from: http://www.gallup-international.com/ContentFiles/survey.asp?id=10 and http://65.109.167.118/pipa/pdf/oct03/IraqMedia_Oct03_rpt.pdf

Gamson, W.A. & Modigliani, A. (July 1989). Media discourse and public opinion on nuclear power: A constructionist approach. *American Journal of Sociology, 95*, 137-177.

Gandy, O.H. (1999). Community pluralism and the "tipping point:" Editorial responses to race and related structural change. In. D. Demers & K. Viswanath (Eds.), *Mass media, social control, and social change: A macrosocial perspective* (pp. 159-181). Ames, Iowa: Iowa State University Press.

Gans, H.L. (1979). *Deciding what's news: A study of CBS evening news, NBC nightly news, 'Newsweek' and 'Time'.* New York: Vintage Books.

Gerbner, G. & Gross, L. (1976). Living with television: The violence profile. *Journal of Communication, 26*, 179.

Gitlin, T. (2003). *The whole world is watching: Mass media in the making and unmaking of the new left.* California, University of California Press.

Goodstein, L. (2001, September 12). A day of terror: The ties: In U.S., echoes of rift of Muslims and Jews. *The New York Times*, pp. 12.

Haberman, C. (2001, August 13). Bombing and shooting of Arab girl deepen fear in Israel. *The New York Times*, pp. 3.

Haberman, C. (2001, August 25). Jews in Hebron only wish that the army would stay. *The New York Times*, pp. 5.

Haigh, M.M., Pfau, M., Danesi, J., Tallmon, R., Bunko, T., Nyberg, S., et al. (2006). A comparison of embedded and nonembedded print coverage of the U.S. invasion and occupation of Iraq. *Press/Politics, 11*(2), 138-152.

Hanley, D.C. (2003). Two wars in Iraq: One for U.S. audiences, the other for the Arabic-speaking world. *The Washington Report on Middle East Affairs, 22*(4), 6.

Haque, A. (2004). Islamophobia in North America. In B. van Driel (Ed.), *Confronting Islamophobia in educational practice* (pp. 1-18). Staffordshire, England: Trentham Books Limited.

Hess, S. & Kalb, M. (2003). *The media and the war on terrorism.* Washington, D.C.: Brookings Institution Press.

Hilsum, L. (2004). The Americans claim to want to nurture reform in the Arab world, yet they ban the tiny Gulf state of Qatar from a meeting on the region because it hosts Al-Jazeera. *New Statesman, 133* (4692), 10.

Iskandar, A. (2005). "The great American bubble:" Fox news channel, the "mirage" of objectivity, and the isolation of American public opinion. In L. Artz and Y.R. Kamalipour (Eds.), *Bring 'em on: Media and politics in the Iraq war* (pp. 155-173). Lanham, Maryland: Rowman & Littlefield Publishers, Inc.

James, C. (2001, October 6). Islam and its adherents ride the publicity wave. *The New York Times*, pp. 8.

Jensen, R. (2005). The problem with patriotism: Steps toward the redemption of American journalism and the democracy. In L. Artz and Y.R. Kamalipour (Eds.), *Bring 'em on: Media and politics in the Iraq war* (pp. 67-83). Lanham, Maryland: Rowman & Littlefield Publishers, Inc.

Josephi, B. (2004). Media terrorism or culture of peace: Reporting September 11. In S. Venkatraman (Ed.), *Media in a terrorized world: Reflections in the wake of 911* (pp. 34-53). Singapore: Eastern Universities Press.

Kahn, J. (2001, September 16). Before & after; Awakening to terror, and asking the world for help. *The New York Times*, pp.12.

Kellner, D. (2004). Spectacle and media propaganda in the war on Iraq: A critique of U.S. broadcasting networks. In Y.R. Kamalipour & N. Snow (Ed.), *War, media, and propaganda: A global perspective.* (pp. 69-77). Lanham, MD: Rowman & Littlefield Publishers, Inc.

Kennedy, D. (2001, September 16). Fighting an elusive enemy. *The New York Times*, pp.11.

La Guardia, A., & Skidelsk, W. (2005). Channel of terror. *New Statesman, 134*(4722), 40-245.

MacFarquhar, N. (2001, September 12). Condemnations from Arab governments, but widely different attitudes on the street. *The New York Times*, pp. 22.

Maslog, C.C., Lee, S.T., & Kim, H.S. (2006, March). Framing analysis of a conflict: How newspapers in five Asian countries covered the Iraq war. *Asian Journal of Communication, 16*(1), 19-39.

McChesney, R.W. (2000). *Rich media, poor democracy: Communication politics in dubious times.* New York, NY: The New Press.

McChesney, R.W. (2005). Global media, neoliberalism, and imperialism. In P. Leistyna (Ed.), *Cultural studies: From theory to action* (pp. 159-170). Malden, MA: Blackwell Publishing Limited.

McFadden, R.D. (2001, September 24). In a stadium of heroes, prayers for the fallen and solace for those left behind. *The New York Times*, pp. 7.

Media and Society Research Group. (2004, December). *MSRG special report: Restrictions on civil liberties, views of Islam, and Muslim Americans.* Cornell University, Ithaca, New York. Retrieved on March 15, 2007 from: http://www.comm.cornell.edu/msrg/report1a.pdf

Media Research Center. (2005, October). *An in-depth study, analysis or review exploring the media: TV's bad news brigade – ABC, CBS, and NBC's defeatist coverage of the war in Iraq.* Retrieved on April 11, 2007 from: http://www.mediaresearch.org/SpecialReports/2005/pdf/TVs_Depressing_Iraq_News .pdf

Montgomerie, D. (2005). Chomsky and Al-Jazeera: Doctrinal control in an emerging democracy. Paper presented at the 2005 CSCA Conference, Kansas City: KC.

MSNBC apology not enough. (2004). *The Arab-American news, 20*(981), 4.

Nacos, B.L. & Torres-Reyna, O. (2003). Framing Muslim-Americans before and after 9/11. In P. Norris, M. Kern & M. Just (Eds.), *Framing terrorism: The news media, the government and the public* (pp. 133-157). New York: Routledge.

Niebuhr,G. (2001, October 6). Ties between a mosque and Fort Bragg stay strong and neighborly. *The New York Times*, pp. 8.

Norris, P., Kern, M., & Just, M. (2003). The lessons of framing terrorism. In P. Norris, M. Kern, & M. Just (Eds.), *Framing terrorism* (pp. 281-302). London, Great Britain: Routledge

Ozanich, G.W. & Wirth, M.O. (2004). Structure and change: A communications industry overview. In A. Alexander, J. Owers, R. Carveth, C.A. Hollifield, & A.N. Greco

(Ed.), *Media economics theory and practices* (pp. 69-84). Mahwah, NJ: Lawrence Erlbaum Associates, Inc., Publishers.

Paletz, D.L. & Entman, R.M. (1981). *Media, power, politics.* New York, NY: The Free Press.

Pan, Z. & Kosicki, G.M. (1993, January - March). Framing analysis: An approach to new discourse. *Political Communication, 10*, 55-75.

Parenti, C. (2004, March 29). Al-Jazeera goes to jail. *Nation, 278*(12), 1-4.

Parenti, M. (1986). *Inventing reality: The politics of the mass media.* New York, NY: St. Martin's Press.

Program on International Policy Attitudes (PIPA) & Knowledge Networks. (2003, October 2). *Misperceptions, the media and the Iraq war.* Retrieved April 10, 2007 from: http://65.109.167.118/pipa/pdf/oct03/IraqMedia_Oct03_rpt.pdf

Public Broadcasting Station. (n. d.) *In focus: This moment in history: Post 9/11 timeline.* Retrieved April 11, 2007 from: http://www.pbs.org/flashpointsusa/20040629/infocus/topic_01/timeline_sep2001.html

Reynolds, A. & Barnett, B. (2003). "America under attack:" CNN's verbal and visual framing of September 11. In S. Chermak, F.Y. Bailey, & M. Brown (Ed.), *Media representations of September 11* (pp. 85-101). Westport, CT: Praeger Publishers.

Richardson, J.E. (2004). *(Mis) representing Islam: The racism and rhetoric of British broadsheet newspapers.* Amsterdam, Netherlands: John Benjamins Publishing Co.

Risen, J. & Johnston, D. (2001, September 12). Officials say they saw no signs of increased terrorist activity. *The New York Times*, pp. 21.

Ross, S.D. & Bantimaroudis, P. (2006). Frame shifts and catastrophic events: The attacks of September 11, 2001, and *New York Times'* portrayals of Arafat and Sharon. *Mass Communication & Society, 9*(1), 85-101.

Rutenberg, J. (2001, October 2). MTV, turning serious, helps its generation cope. *The New York Times*, pp. 1.

Sachs, S. (2001, September 28). Pop star and public officials join campaign for tolerance. *The New York Times*, pp. 27.

Schecter, D. (2004). Selling the Iraq war: the media management strategies we never saw. In Y.R. Kamalipour & N. Snow (Ed.), *War, media, and propaganda: A global perspective* (pp. 25-32). Lanham, MD: Rowman & Littlefield Publishers, Inc.

Shaheen, J.G. (2001). *Reel bad Arabs: How Hollywood vilifies a people.* New York: Olive Branch Press.

Shanahan, J. (2004). A return to cultural indicators. *Communications: The European Journal of Communication Research, 29,* 277-294.

Shanahan, J. & Morgan, M. (1999). *Television and its viewers: Cultivation theory and research.* Cambridge, UK: Cambridge University Press.

Sheler, J.L., & Betzold, M. (2001). Muslims in America. *U.S. News & World Report, 131*(18), 48-53.

Sheridan, L. (2004). Islamophobia before and after September 11th, 2001. In B. van Driel (Ed.), *Confronting Islamophobia in educational practice* (pp. 163-176). Staffordshire, England: Trentham Books Limited.

Shoemaker, P.J. (1984). Media treatment of deviant political groups. *Journalism Quarterly, 61,* 66-75.

Smith, D. (2005, April 25). The enemy on our airwaves. The *Wall Street Journal*, pp.14.

Staggenborg, S. (1993). Critical events and the mobilization of the pro-choice movement. *Research in Political Sociology, 6,* 319-45.

Stempel, G.H. & Hargrove, T. (2002). Media sources of information and attitudes about terrorism. In B.S. Greenberg (Ed.), *Communication and terrorism: Public and media responses to 9/11* (pp. 17-26). Cresskill, NJ: Hampton Press, Inc.

Tankard, J., Hendrickson, L., Silberman, J., Bliss, K., & Ghanem, S. (1991, August). *Media frames: Approaches to conceptualization and measurement.* Annual convention of the association of education in journalism and mass communication, Boston, MA.

U.S. seeks to curb Al-Jazeera's freedom of speech. (2001). The *Arab-American News, 18*(817), 9.

Van Driel, B. (2004). Introduction. In B. van Driel (Ed.), *Confronting Islamophobia in educational practice* (pp. vii-xiii). Staffordshire, England: Trentham Books Limited.

Vergeer, M., Lubbers, M., & Scheepers, P. (2000). Exposure to newspapers and attitudes toward ethnic minorities: A longitudinal analysis. *The Howard Journal of Communication, 11*, 127-43.

Vivian, J. (2005). *The media of mass communication* (7th Ed.).Boston, MA: Allyn and Bacon.

Yumul, A. (2004). Mediating the 'Other' through advertisements. In T. Parfitt (Ed.), *Jews, Muslims and mass media* (pp. 35-47). London: Routledge Curzon.

www.ingramcontent.com/pod-product-compliance
Lightning Source LLC
Chambersburg PA
CBHW072155020426
42334CB00018B/2011